Dec 15/21

ROAST

THE AUSTRALIAN
Women's Weekly

ROAST
classic + contemporary

acp
books

contents

The word *roast* brings to mind images of Sundays, family, and flavoursome comfort food. The roast is a sure-fire crowd-pleaser, and by putting the tips and recipes in this book into action you'll have perfect results every time. Roast potatoes are an absolute favourite. Make them crispy golden on the outside and soft on the inside by par-boiling them, then scratching the surface with a fork and tossing in a roasting pan with a thin layer of olive oil. To test if your roast is cooked, run a fine skewer into the thickest part of the meat. For red meat, the juices will be red when cooked to rare, pink for medium-rare and clear for well-done. Seafood is cooked when it changes from translucent to opaque; a whole fish is done when a toothpick is inserted without resistance. For poultry, the juices should run clear, without a trace of pink. Protect wings or legs of poultry by covering them in foil.

To achieve the most succulent result, "rest" meat and poultry after it is cooked. Stand, covered, in a warm place for 5 minutes for small pieces or 15 minutes for large pieces. With family and friends around, and a delicious, warm roast on the table, things couldn't be better. Enjoy.

poultry

Citrus chicken with vermicelli salad

4 chicken marylands (1.4kg)
¼ cup (60ml) lemon juice
2 fresh small red thai chillies, sliced thinly
2 cloves garlic, crushed
¼ cup (85g) orange marmalade
250g rice vermicelli
2 medium oranges (480g)
1 medium lebanese cucumber (130g), seeded, sliced thinly crossways
⅔ cup loosely packed fresh mint leaves
citrus dressing
2 tablespoons lemon juice
2 tablespoons orange marmalade
2 teaspoons vegetable oil

1 Pierce chicken all over with skewer. Combine chicken, juice, chilli, garlic and marmalade in large bowl. Cover; refrigerate 3 hours or overnight.
2 Preheat oven to 200°C/180°C fan-forced.
3 Place drained chicken on oiled wire rack in large shallow baking dish; reserve marinade. Roast, uncovered, about 45 minutes or until cooked through, brushing occasionally with reserved marinade.
4 Meanwhile, place vermicelli in large heatproof bowl, cover with boiling water. Stand until just tender; drain. Rinse vermicelli under cold water; drain. Using scissors, cut vermicelli into random lengths.
5 Segment oranges over small bowl; reserve 2 teaspoons of juice.
6 Make citrus dressing.
7 Place vermicelli and orange segments in large bowl with cucumber, mint and dressing; toss gently to combine. Serve salad with chicken.
citrus dressing place ingredients and reserved orange juice in screw-top jar; shake well.

preparation time 15 minutes (plus refrigeration time)
cooking time 45 minutes **serves** 4
nutritional count per serving 36.1g total fat (10.9g saturated fat); 3520kJ (842 cal); 75.0g carbohydrate; 51.1g protein; 4.8g fibre

Lemon thyme roast chicken

1.8kg whole chicken
40g butter
1 large brown onion (200g), chopped finely
2 cloves garlic, crushed
4 rashers rindless bacon (260g), chopped finely
1 egg, beaten lightly
1½ cups (105g) stale breadcrumbs
1 tablespoon chopped fresh lemon thyme
80g butter, extra, softened
¼ teaspoon sea salt flakes
12 small carrots (840g)

1 Preheat oven to 200°C/180°C fan-forced. Oil large flameproof roasting dish.
2 Wash chicken and pat dry with absorbent paper.
3 Heat butter in medium frying pan; cook onion, garlic and bacon, stirring, until onion is soft. Remove from heat; cool 5 minutes.
4 Combine bacon mixture, egg, breadcrumbs and 2 teaspoons of thyme in medium bowl. Fill cavity of chicken with seasoning.
5 Combine extra butter and 1 teaspoon of the remaining thyme in small bowl. Carefully separate the skin from the breast of chicken with your fingers; spread herb butter under skin covering breast. Secure skin over cavity with toothpicks. Tie legs together with kitchen string; tuck wings underneath. Rub remaining thyme and salt over skin.
6 Place chicken in baking dish; roast, uncovered, for 20 minutes. Add carrots; roast further 40 minutes or until chicken is cooked through. Stand, covered, for 10 minutes. Remove and discard tothpicks.
7 Sprinkle chicken with extra thyme leaves and salt, if desired. Serve with carrots.

preparation time 20 minutes **cooking time** 1 hour 10 minutes (plus cooling and standing times) **serves** 4
nutritional count per serving 71.9g total fat (31.3g saturated fat); 4335kJ (1037 cal); 30.3g carbohydrate; 65.1g protein; 7.3g fibre

Sticky drumettes with roasted root vegies

1 medium kumara (400g), cut into wedges
300g kipfler potatoes, cut into wedges
1 large parsnip (350g), cut into wedges
2 tablespoons olive oil
1 tablespoon chopped fresh rosemary
3 cloves garlic, crushed
20 chicken drumettes (1.4kg)
1 ½ teaspoons sweet paprika
1 tablespoon coarse cooking salt
2 teaspoons caster sugar
½ teaspoon ground black pepper
½ teaspoon ground lemon myrtle
¼ teaspoon ground cinnamon
2 tablespoons maple syrup

1 Preheat oven to 220°C/200°C fan-forced.
2 Combine vegetables, oil, rosemary and garlic in large shallow baking dish. Roast, uncovered, in single layer, about 35 minutes or until vegetables are just tender.
3 Meanwhile, combine drumettes and remaining ingredients in large bowl. Place drumettes, in single layer, on oiled wire rack in large shallow baking dish; roast, uncovered, with vegetables about 30 minutes or until cooked through.
4 Serve drumettes with roasted vegetables.

preparation time 20 minutes **cooking time** 35 minutes **serves** 4
nutritional count per serving 30.5g total fat (7.7g saturated fat);
2483kJ (594 cal); 40.0g carbohydrate; 38.2g protein; 4.9g fibre

Pepper-roasted garlic and lemon chicken

2 bulbs garlic
2kg whole chicken
cooking-oil spray
2 teaspoons salt
2 tablespoons cracked black pepper
1 medium lemon (140g), cut into eight wedges
1 cup (250ml) water
3 medium globe artichokes (660g)
2 tablespoons lemon juice
2 medium red onions (340g), quartered
3 baby fennel bulbs (390g), trimmed, halved
2 medium leeks (700g), halved lengthways then quartered
250g cherry tomatoes
⅓ cup (80ml) dry white wine
¼ cup (60ml) lemon juice, extra

1 Preheat oven to 200°C/180°C fan-forced.
2 Separate cloves from garlic bulb, leaving skin intact. Wash chicken under cold water; pat dry inside and out with absorbent paper. Coat chicken with cooking-oil spray; press combined salt and pepper onto skin and inside cavity. Place garlic and lemon inside cavity; tie legs together with kitchen string. Place chicken on small oiled wire rack in large flameproof baking dish, pour the water in baking dish; roast, uncovered, 50 minutes.
3 Meanwhile, discard outer leaves from artichokes; cut tips from remaining leaves. Trim then peel stalks. Quarter artichokes lengthways; using teaspoon remove chokes. Cover artichoke with cold water in medium bowl, stir in the 2 tablespoons of lemon juice; soak until required.
4 Add drained artichoke, onion, fennel and leek to dish; coat with cooking-oil spray. Roast, uncovered, 40 minutes or until vegetables are just tender.
5 Add tomatoes to dish; roast, uncovered, about 20 minutes or until tomatoes soften and chicken is cooked through. Place chicken on serving dish and vegetables in large bowl; cover to keep warm.
6 Stir wine and extra juice into dish with pan juices; bring to the boil. Boil 2 minutes then strain sauce over vegetables; toss gently to combine.
7 Discard garlic and lemon from cavity; serve chicken with vegetables.

preparation time 35 minutes **cooking time** 1 hour 50 minutes **serves** 4
nutritional count per serving 35.7g total fat (10.7g saturated fat); 2859kJ (684 cal); 18.8g carbohydrate; 62.0g protein; 14.6g fibre

Roasted spicy chicken drumsticks with kumara chips

12 chicken drumsticks (1.8kg)
⅔ cup (200g) yogurt
2 cloves garlic, crushed
1 tablespoon ground cumin
1 tablespoon ground coriander
2 tablespoons finely chopped fresh mint
2 small kumara (500g)
vegetable oil, for deep-frying

1 Preheat oven to 220°C/200°C fan-forced.
2 Combine drumsticks, yogurt, garlic, cumin, coriander and mint in large bowl.
3 Place chicken, in single layer, in large shallow oiled baking dish. Roast, uncovered, 20 minutes. Using metal tongs, turn chicken; spoon pan liquid over each drumstick then roast, uncovered, further 20 minutes or until chicken is cooked through.
4 Meanwhile, using vegetable peeler, slice peeled kumara into long, thin ribbons. Heat oil in medium frying pan; deep-fry kumara, in batches, until lightly browned. Drain on absorbent paper.
5 Serve chicken with kumara chips.

preparation time 20 minutes **cooking time** 40 minutes **serves** 4
nutritional count per serving 40.1g total fat (11.5g saturated fat); 2725kJ (652 cal); 17.6g carbohydrate; 54.6g protein; 2.3g fibre
tips chicken wings can be substituted for drumsticks. Buy large wings: 12 of these will weigh about 1.5kg and be enough to serve four people adequately. Chicken can be marinated in the yogurt mixture overnight and refrigerated, covered.

Slow-roasted portuguese chicken

Sometimes known as piri-piri chicken after Portugal's favourite spicy hot sauce, this style of cooking chicken has become a runaway success, winning customers from traditional deep-fried, spit-roast or barbecued chicken shops.

1.6kg whole chicken
1 fresh small red thai chilli, seeded, chopped finely
1 tablespoon sweet paprika
3 cloves garlic, crushed
2 teaspoons salt
½ cup (125ml) lemon juice
2 tablespoons olive oil
1 tablespoon coarsely chopped fresh oregano

1 Preheat oven to 160°C/140°C fan-forced.
2 Wash chicken under cold running water; pat dry with absorbent paper. Using kitchen scissors, cut along both sides of backbone; discard backbone. Place chicken, skin-side up, on board; using heel of hand, press down on breastbone to flatten chicken. Insert metal skewer through thigh and opposite wing of chicken to keep chicken flat. Repeat with other thigh and wing.
3 Combine remaining ingredients in small bowl.
4 Place chicken in large baking dish; pour chilli mixture over chicken. Roast, uncovered, brushing occasionally with pan juices, about 2 hours or until chicken is browned and cooked through. Remove skewers. Serve with roast vegetables, if desired.

preparation time 15 minutes **cooking time** 2 hours **serves** 4
nutritional count per serving 41.4g total fat (11.3g saturated fat); 2232kJ (534 cal); 1.1g carbohydrate; 40.3g protein; 0.4g fibre
tips add one or two more chillies to the spice mixture for a hotter flavour. If desired, marinate chicken in chilli mixture, covered, in the refrigerator, overnight; turning constantly to coat each side. You can use chicken pieces rather than a whole chicken if you prefer: try a mixture of whole thighs and drumsticks, marylands or whole breasts… just remember to reduce the cooking time.

Prosciutto-wrapped spatchcocks with lemon and sage

8 x 500g spatchcocks
1 medium lemon (140g), cut into eight wedges
16 fresh sage leaves
8 thin slices (120g) prosciutto
2 medium lemons (280g), extra
fennel rub
1 teaspoon fennel seeds, toasted, crushed
1 clove garlic, crushed
2 tablespoons olive oil

1 Preheat oven to 220°C/200°C fan-forced.
2 Wash spatchcocks under cold water; clean cavity well. Pat dry inside and out with absorbent paper.
3 Place a lemon wedge and two sage leaves into each spatchcock cavity.
4 Combine ingredients for fennel rub in small bowl; rub the mixture all over the spatchcocks.
5 Wrap the centre of each spatchcock with a slice of prosciutto; secure with a toothpick.
6 Divide the spatchcocks between two baking dishes. Roast, uncovered, about 45 minutes or until browned and cooked through. Transfer to a serving platter; cover with foil to keep warm. Stand for 15 minutes. Remove and discard toothpicks.
7 Serve spatchcocks with extra lemon wedges, if desired.

preparation time 20 minutes
cooking time 45 minutes (plus standing time) **serves** 8
nutritional count per serving 44.9g total fat (13.3g saturated fat); 2546kJ (609 cal); 0.3g carbohydrate; 51.8g protein; 0.3g fibre
tip spatchcocks can be prepared several hours ahead; roast close to serving time.

Roast goose with fruit and nut seasoning

20g butter, melted
1 tablespoon honey
1 teaspoon light soy sauce
3.5kg whole goose
1 tablespoon plain flour
fruit and nut seasoning
2 tablespoons vegetable oil
200g chicken giblets, chopped finely
1 medium brown onion (150g), chopped finely
1 trimmed celery stalk (100g), chopped finely
1 medium apple (150g), chopped finely
½ cup (80g) coarsely chopped brazil nuts
½ cup (70g) slivered almonds
½ cup (75g) coarsely chopped dried apricots
½ cup (85g) finely chopped raisins
1 tablespoon chopped fresh mint
1½ cups (100g) stale breadcrumbs

1 Preheat oven to 200°C/180°C fan-forced.
2 Make fruit and nut seasoning.
3 Combine butter, honey and sauce in small bowl, brush mixture inside and outside of goose. Fill goose with seasoning, secure opening with skewers. Tie legs together, tuck wings under goose. Prick skin to release fat during roasting.
4 Lightly flour large oven bag; place goose in bag, secure with tie provided. Make holes in bag as advised on package. Place goose breast-side up in baking dish, cover dish with foil; roast 1 hour. Remove foil, roast goose further 1 hour. Remove and discard skewers.
fruit and nut seasoning Heat half the oil in medium saucepan; cook giblets, stirring, until browned; drain on absorbent paper. Add remaining oil to pan; cook onion and celery, stirring, until onion is soft. Add apple and nuts; cook, stirring, until nuts are browned lightly. Remove from heat, stir in giblets, apricots, raisins, mint and breadcrumbs; cool.

preparation time 1 hour **cooking time** 2 hours 15 minutes
serves 8
nutritional count per serving 113.0g total fat (32.2g saturated fat); 5405kJ (1293 cal); 27.0g carbohydrate; 43.4g protein; 4.3g fibre

Soy duck breasts with noodles

6 single duck breast fillets (950g)
½ cup (125ml) chinese cooking wine
½ cup (125ml) soy sauce
4cm piece fresh ginger (20g), grated
3 cloves garlic, crushed
1 tablespoon white sugar
2 fresh long red chillies, chopped
600g gai lan, chopped
450g thin fresh hokkien noodles

1 Score the skin and fat of duck breasts through to the flesh.
2 Place duck in large bowl with combined wine, soy sauce, ginger, garlic, sugar and chilli. Cover; refrigerate 1 hour.
3 Preheat oven grill to 240°C/220°C fan-forced.
4 Drain duck from marinade; reserve marinade. Place duck breasts, skin-side up, on oiled wire rack over shallow baking dish. Grill 6 minutes or until skin is browned and crisp. Turn, cook a further 3 minutes or until cooked as desired. Stand 5 minutes.
5 Meanwhile, boil, steam or microwave gai lan until just tender; drain.
6 Place reserved marinade in saucepan; bring to the boil. Reduce heat; simmer, uncovered 1 minute.
7 Place noodles in heatproof bowl, cover with boiling water. Stand for 2 minutes, then separate noodles with a fork; drain.
8 Serve duck on noodles and gai lan; drizzle with hot marinade.

preparation time 30 minutes (plus refrigeration time)
cooking time 10 minutes (plus standing time) **serves** 6
nutritional count per serving 13.5g total fat (4.8g saturated fat); 1693kJ (405 cal); 23.4g carbohydrate; 39.0g protein; 6.3g fibre

Southern fried chicken with buttermilk mash and gravy

20 chicken drumettes (1.4kg)
1 cup (250ml) buttermilk
1 cup (150g) plain flour
¼ cup cajun seasoning
½ cup (125ml) vegetable oil
40g butter
5 medium potatoes (1kg), chopped coarsely
¾ cup (180ml) buttermilk, warmed, extra
40g butter, extra
250g green beans, trimmed, cut into 4cm lengths
2 cups (500ml) chicken stock

1 Combine chicken and buttermilk in large bowl. Cover; refrigerate 3 hours or overnight. Drain; discard buttermilk.
2 Combine flour and seasoning in large bowl; add chicken, toss to coat in mixture. Cover; refrigerate about 30 minutes or until flour forms a paste.
3 Preheat oven to 240°C/220°C fan-forced.
4 Heat oil and butter in large deep frying pan; shake excess paste from chicken back into bowl. Cook chicken, in batches, over medium heat until browned and crisp.
5 Place chicken on oiled wire rack over large baking dish; roast, covered, in oven 15 minutes. Uncover; roast about 10 minutes or until chicken is cooked through and crisp.
6 Meanwhile, boil, steam or microwave potato until tender; drain. Mash with extra buttermilk and extra butter until smooth. Cover to keep warm.
7 Boil, steam or microwave beans until tender; drain.
8 To make gravy, add excess paste to pan; cook, stirring, until mixture bubbles. Gradually stir in stock; cook, stirring, until gravy boils and thickens. Strain gravy into large jug.
9 Serve chicken with mash, beans and gravy.

preparation time 20 minutes (plus refrigeration time)
cooking time 40 minutes **serves** 4
nutritional count per serving 69.7g total fat (22.6g saturated fat); 4585kJ (1097 cal); 64.3g carbohydrate; 50.4g protein; 6.6g fibre
tip cajun seasoning is available from the spice section at the supermarket.

Spiced roasted spatchcocks with coriander

4 x 500g spatchcocks
4 cloves garlic, peeled
4cm piece fresh ginger (20g), grated
⅓ cup (40g) almond meal
¼ cup (60ml) lemon juice
3 fresh coriander roots
½ teaspoon ground turmeric
3 teaspoons garam masala
3 fresh large green chillies, chopped coarsely
2 teaspoons salt
30g ghee, melted
¼ cup firmly packed fresh coriander leaves

1 Place spatchcocks on a board, cut down both sides of the backbones with poultry shears or sharp knife; remove and discard the backbones. Rinse the cavities of spatchcocks and pat dry. Place each spatchcock, breast-side up, on board; press the breastbone firmly with the heel of hand to flatten.
2 Blend or process garlic, ginger, almond meal, juice, roots, turmeric, garam masala, chilli and salt until combined. Rub spice mixture over spatchcocks; cover, refrigerate 3 hours or overnight.
3 Preheat oven to 240°C/220°C fan-forced.
4 Place spatchcocks on an oiled wire rack over large, shallow flameproof baking dish; brush with ghee. Roast, uncovered, about 30 minutes or until browned all over and cooked through.
5 Serve spatchcocks with coriander and lemon wedges, if desired.

preparation time 20 minutes (plus refrigeration time)
cooking time 30 minutes **serves** 4
nutritional count per serving 52.6g total fat (17.6g saturated fat); 2859kJ (684 cal); 1.5g carbohydrate; 51.5g protein; 1.7g fibre

Classic roast chicken

40g butter
2 rashers rindless bacon (130g), chopped finely
1 small leek (200g), sliced thinly
2 trimmed celery stalks (200g), chopped finely
2 cups (140g) stale breadcrumbs
1 egg, beaten lightly
1 tablespoon coarsely chopped fresh sage
1.8kg whole chicken
2 tablespoons olive oil
6 medium potatoes (1kg), halved
2 tablespoons plain flour
2 cups (500ml) chicken stock
1 cup (250ml) water

1 Melt butter in medium frying pan; cook bacon, leek and celery until vegetables are tender, cool. Combine bacon mixture in medium bowl with breadcrumbs, egg and sage.
2 Preheat oven to 200°C/180°C fan-forced.
3 Wash chicken under cold running water; pat dry inside and out with absorbent paper. Tuck wing tips under chicken. Trim skin around neck; secure to underside of chicken with toothpicks.
4 Fill cavity with bacon mixture; tie legs together with string. Place chicken on oiled wire rack in large flameproof baking dish. Rub chicken all over with half of the oil; roast, uncovered, 1½ hours.
5 Meanwhile, boil, steam or microwave potato 5 minutes; drain. Combine potato and remaining oil in large shallow baking dish; roast, uncovered, alongside chicken 1 hour, turning occasionally during roasting. Remove chicken from oven; cover to keep warm. Remove and discard toothpicks.
6 Increase oven temperature to 240°C/220°C fan-forced. Roast potato, uncovered, further 15 minutes or until browned and crisp.
7 Meanwhile, drain all but 2 tablespoons of the juices from chicken dish, add flour; cook, stirring over medium heat, until mixture thickens and bubbles. Gradually add combined stock and the water, stirring until gravy boils and thickens. Strain into large jug. Serve with chicken and potatoes.

preparation time 20 minutes
cooking time 1 hour 30 minutes (plus cooling time) **serves** 4
nutritional count per serving 61.3g total fat (20.5g saturated fat); 4320kJ (1046 cal); 56.0g carbohydrate; 65.3g protein; 6.5g fibre

Boned turkey buffé with couscous stuffing

½ cup (80g) sultanas
½ cup (125ml) lemon juice
4.5kg butterflied turkey buffé (order from the butcher)
1 litre (4 cups) chicken stock
¼ cup (60ml) olive oil
1 cup (200g) couscous
¼ cup (40g) toasted pepitas
¼ cup (35g) roasted slivered almonds
¼ cup (35g) roasted pecans, chopped coarsely
¼ cup coarsely chopped fresh flat-leaf parsley
¼ cup coarsely chopped fresh coriander
2 eggs, beaten lightly
1 litre (4 cups) water
½ cup (125ml) dry white wine
⅓ cup (50g) plain flour

1 Soak sultanas in small bowl in half of the juice. Make paprika rub.
2 Preheat oven to 180°C/160°C fan-forced.
3 Place turkey flat on board, skin-side down; cover with plastic wrap.
Using rolling pin or meat mallet, flatten turkey meat to an even thickness.
4 Bring 1 cup of the stock, oil and remaining juice to the boil in large
saucepan. Stir in couscous, cover; stand 5 minutes. Stir in sultana mixture,
pepitas, nuts, herbs and egg.
5 With pointed end of turkey facing away from you, place stuffing in centre.
Bring pointed end over stuffing, securing to neck skin with toothpicks.
Working from centre out, continue securing sides of turkey with
toothpicks (to form a rectangle). Tie with kitchen string at 4cm intervals.
6 Place turkey on wire rack in large baking dish; add 1 cup of the water
and wine to dish. Rub turkey with paprika rub; cover dish with oiled foil.
Roast 1 hour. Uncover; roast further 45 minutes. Remove and discard
toothpicks. Transfer to platter; cover.
7 Stir flour into juices in dish; cook, stirring, until well browned. Stir in
remaining stock and remaining water; stir until gravy boils and thickens.
Strain into large jug; serve with turkey.
paprika rub Using mortar and pestle, crush 1 teaspoon each of fennel
seeds and sweet paprika, with ½ teaspoon ground ginger, 2 teaspoons
salt, 2 cloves chopped garlic and 2 tablespoons olive oil until smooth.
preparation time 1 hour **cooking time** 2 hours **serves** 10
nutritional count per serving 32.3g total fat (6.6g saturated fat);
3344kJ (800 cal); 26.4g carbohydrate; 97.4g protein; 1.8g fibre

Caramelised chicken cutlets

2 teaspoons vegetable oil
4 chicken thigh cutlets (800g), skin on
1 medium red onion (170g), sliced thinly
3 cloves garlic, sliced thinly
¼ cup (55g) brown sugar
1 tablespoon dark soy sauce
1 tablespoon fish sauce
⅓ cup coarsely chopped fresh coriander

1 Preheat oven to 200°C/180°C fan-forced.
2 Heat oil in large frying pan; cook chicken, both sides, until browned.
Place chicken, in single layer, in baking dish. Roast, uncovered, in oven,
about 25 minutes or until cooked through.
3 Meanwhile, heat same frying pan; cook onion and garlic, stirring,
until onion softens. Add sugar and sauces; cook, stirring, 3 minutes.
Return chicken to pan with coriander; turn chicken to coat in mixture.

preparation time 20 minutes **cooking time** 35 minutes **serves** 4
nutritional count per serving 22.4g total fat (6.9g saturated fat);
1538kJ (368 cal); 16.3g carbohydrate; 24.8g protein; 1.0g fibre

Saffron chicken on potatoes

1.8kg whole chicken
1kg nicola or desiree potatoes, cut into 5mm slices
8 cloves garlic, unpeeled
¼ cup (60ml) extra virgin olive oil
6 sprigs fresh thyme
1 tablespoon sea salt flakes
1 teaspoon freshly ground black pepper
¼ teaspoon saffron threads
2 tablespoons extra virgin olive oil, extra

1 Preheat oven to 220°C/200°C fan-forced.
2 Wash chicken under cold running water; pat dry with absorbent paper. Using kitchen scissors, cut along both sides of backbone; discard backbone. Place chicken, skin-side up, on board; using heel of hand, press down on breastbone to flatten chicken.
3 Place potatoes in a large baking dish with six of the garlic cloves, oil, thyme, half the salt and pepper; toss to combine.
4 Blend or process remaining garlic with saffron, remaining salt and pepper and extra oil.
5 Carefully separate skin from chicken breast with fingers. Place a tablespoon of saffron mixture under skin; rub into flesh. Rub remaining mixture all over chicken; place chicken on top of potatoes.
6 Roast, uncovered, about 1 hour 10 minutes or until chicken is cooked through and potatoes are golden brown.

preparation time 20 minutes **cooking time** 1 hour 10 minutes
serves 4
nutritional count per serving 59.3g total fat (14.5g saturated fat); 3528kJ (844 cal); 26.8g carbohydrate; 50.1g protein; 4.2g fibre

Roasted chicken with 40 cloves of garlic

This moreish Provençal favourite will surprise you with how mild and creamy the garlic becomes after its long roasting. Feel free to use as many cloves as you want because any leftover roasted garlic cloves can be peeled and used to make a simple garlic mayonnaise known as aïoli.

3 bulbs garlic
60g butter, softened
1.5kg whole chicken
2 teaspoons salt
2 teaspoons cracked black pepper
1 cup (250ml) water
roasted potatoes
1kg baby new potatoes
cooking-oil spray

1 Preheat oven to 200°C/180°C fan-forced.
2 Separate cloves from garlic bulb, leaving peel intact. Rub butter over outside of chicken and inside cavity; press combined salt and pepper onto skin and inside cavity. Place half of the garlic inside cavity; tie legs together with kitchen string.
3 Place remaining garlic cloves, in single layer, in medium baking dish; place chicken on garlic. Pour the water carefully into dish; roast, uncovered, brushing occasionally with pan juices, about 1 hour 20 minutes or until browned and cooked through.
4 Meanwhile, make roasted potatoes.
5 Stand chicken on platter, covered with foil, 15 minutes before serving with roasted garlic and potatoes.

roasted potatoes boil steam or microwave potatoes 5 minutes; drain. Pat dry with absorbent paper; cool 10 minutes. Place potatoes, in single layer, in large oiled baking dish; spray with cooking-oil spray. Roast alongside chicken for the last 30 minutes of its cooking time or until potatoes are tender.

preparation time 20 minutes
cooking time 1 hour 20 minutes (plus standing time) **serves** 4
nutritional count per serving 45.0g total fat (17.9g saturated fat); 3219kJ (770 cal); 38.4g carbohydrate; 46.8g protein; 14.1g fibre

Lemon thyme and chilli roast spatchcock

4 x 500g spatchcocks, quartered
1 tablespoon fresh lemon thyme leaves
lemon thyme and chilli marinade
2 fresh long red chillies, chopped finely
2 cloves garlic, crushed
1 tablespoon fresh lemon thyme leaves
2 teaspoons finely grated lemon rind
¼ cup (60ml) lemon juice
2 tablespoons olive oil
2 tablespoons balsamic vinegar
2 tablespoons honey

1 Make lemon thyme and chilli marinade.
2 Combine three-quarters of the marinade with spatchcock in large shallow dish. Cover; refrigerate 3 hours or overnight. Reserve remaining marinade; refrigerate until required.
3 Preheat oven to 220°C/200°C fan-forced.
4 Place spatchcock, in single layer, on oiled wire racks in large shallow baking dishes. Roast, uncovered, about 40 minutes or until cooked.
5 Serve spatchcock drizzled with reserved marinade and sprinkled with thyme leaves.
lemon thyme and chilli marinade place ingredients in screw-top jar; shake well.

preparation time 30 minutes (plus refrigeration time)
cooking time 40 minutes **serves** 4
nutritional count per serving 48.7g total fat (13.6g saturated fat); 2838kJ (679 cal); 11.8g carbohydrate; 49.3g protein; 0.4g fibre

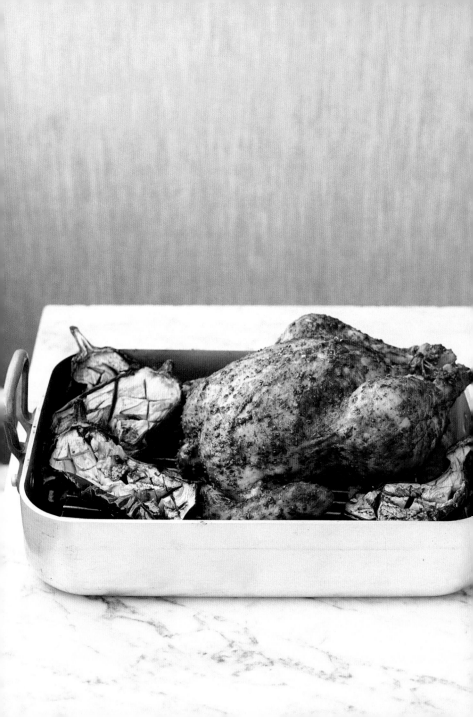

Spiced chicken roasted with eggplant

1½ teaspoons coriander seeds
¾ teaspoon cumin seeds
1 teaspoon black peppercorns
1½ teaspoons sea salt flakes
¾ teaspoon chilli powder
½ teaspoon ground cinnamon
1 tablespoon plain flour
1 tablespoon olive oil
2kg whole chicken
1 medium lemon, halved
1 cup (250ml) chicken stock
2 large eggplants (1kg), halved, scored deeply
⅓ cup coarsely chopped fresh flat-leaf parsley

1 Preheat oven to 180°C/160°C fan-forced.
2 Using a mortar and pestle or small spice mill, crush coriander, cumin, peppercorns and salt until finely ground. Transfer to small bowl, add chilli powder, cinnamon, flour and oil. Rub spice mixture evenly all over chicken.
3 Squeeze lemon and reserve 1 tablespoon of the juice. Stuff the lemon halves into the cavity of the chicken. Tie legs of chicken together; tuck wings under the body. Place chicken on large oiled wire rack in baking dish. Add stock to dish; cover tightly with foil. Roast 20 minutes.
4 Add eggplant to same baking dish; roast, uncovered, further 1 hour.
5 Transfer chicken to serving dish; cover to keep warm. Carefully scoop eggplant flesh into medium bowl; stir in parsley and reserved lemon juice until combined.
6 Serve chicken with warm eggplant mixture and extra lemon, if desired.

preparation time 25 minutes   **cooking time** 1 hour 20 minutes
serves 6
nutritional count per serving 30.5g total fat (8.9g saturated fat);
1877kJ (449 cal); 6.2g carbohydrate; 35.9g protein; 4.4g fibre

Roast bacon-wrapped quail with muscat sauce

Muscat is a sweet, aromatic dessert wine, possessing an almost musty flavour. It is made from the fully matured muscatel grape.

4 quails (780g)
1 medium lemon (140g)
20g butter
4 rashers rindless bacon (260g)
⅓ cup (80ml) muscat
250g green beans
½ cup (125ml) chicken stock
150g fresh muscatel grapes, halved

1 Preheat oven to 200°C/180°C fan-forced.
2 Discard necks from quails. Wash quails under cold water; pat dry with absorbent paper.
3 Halve lemon; cut one lemon half into four wedges. Place one lemon wedge and a quarter of the butter inside each quail. Tuck legs along body, wrapping tightly with bacon rasher to hold legs in place.
4 Place quails in medium flameproof baking dish; drizzle with combined 1 tablespoon of the muscat and juice of remaining lemon half. Roast, uncovered, about 25 minutes or until quails are browned and cooked through. Remove quails from dish; cover to keep warm.
5 Meanwhile, boil, steam or microwave beans until tender; drain. Cover to keep warm.
6 Return dish with pan liquid to heat, add remaining muscat and stock; stir until sauce boils and reduces to about ½ cup. Add grapes; stir until heated though. Serve quail on beans topped with muscat sauce.

preparation time 15 minutes **cooking time** 30 minutes **serves** 4
nutritional count per serving 23.8g total fat (8.8g saturated fat); 1676kJ (401 cal); 9.4g carbohydrate; 33.0g protein; 2.6g fibre

Slow-roasted turkey with port gravy

4kg whole turkey
¼ cup (60ml) chicken stock
½ cup (125ml) port
2 tablespoons brown sugar
2 tablespoons vegetable oil
2 tablespoons plain flour
seasoning
2 tablespoons vegetable oil
2 medium brown onions (300g), sliced thinly
500g sausage mince
4 cups (280g) stale breadcrumbs
2 tablespoons chopped fresh sage
½ cup (60g) chopped walnuts

1 Preheat oven to 150°C/130°C fan-forced.
2 Make seasoning.
3 Discard neck and giblets from turkey. Rinse turkey under cold water; pat dry inside and out with absorbent paper, tuck wings under body. Spoon seasoning loosely into cavity. Tie legs together with kitchen string.
4 Place turkey into oiled flameproof baking dish; pour stock and half of the port into dish. Cover tightly with oiled foil (if thin, use two layers); roast for 5½ hours. Remove foil; brush turkey with combined remaining port and sugar. Increase oven temperature to 180°C/160°C fan-forced; roast, uncovered, further 30 minutes or until browned. Remove turkey from dish; cover with foil to keep warm.
5 Strain juices from dish into jug; remove fat. You will need 3 cups (750ml) pan juices. Heat oil in same baking dish, stir in flour; stir over heat until well browned. Remove from heat, gradually stir in reserved pan juices; stir over heat until gravy boils and thickens, strain.
6 Serve turkey with gravy and, if desired, pumpkin and steamed beans.
seasoning heat oil in large frying pan; cook onion, stirring, until browned. Cool. Transfer onion to medium bowl; stir in remaining ingredients.

preparation time 30 minutes
cooking time 6 hours 10 minutes (plus cooling time) **serves** 8
nutritional count per serving 62.1g total fat (17.6g saturated fat); 4105kJ (982 cal); 34.2g carbohydrate; 67.2g protein; 3.6g fibre

Harissa-roasted chicken and veg

1 small orange (180g), cut into thin wedges
1.6kg whole chicken
1 tablespoon olive oil
300g baby onions
1 bulb garlic, separated into cloves, unpeeled
500g baby new potatoes
4 baby eggplants (240g), halved lengthways
250g cherry tomatoes
harissa
⅓ cup (15g) dried red chillies, chopped coarsely
½ teaspoon ground cumin
½ teaspoon ground coriander
½ teaspoon caraway seeds
1 clove garlic, quartered
1 tablespoon tomato paste
2 teaspoons finely grated orange rind
¼ cup (60ml) orange juice

1 Make harissa.
2 Preheat oven to 180°C/160°C fan-forced.
3 Place orange inside cavity of chicken. Make a pocket between breast and skin with fingers; rub 2 tablespoons of the harissa under skin inside pocket. Tie legs together with kitchen string; brush chicken all over with 2 tablespoons of the harissa.
4 Half-fill large shallow baking dish with water; place chicken on oiled wire rack over dish. Roast, uncovered, about 1 hour. Cover; roast, further 50 minutes or until chicken is cooked through.
5 Meanwhile, heat oil in large flameproof baking dish; cook onions, garlic and potatoes, stirring, until vegetables are browned. Add eggplant and tomatoes; roast in oven for the last 20 minutes of chicken cooking time or until vegetables are tender. Serve with chicken and remaining harissa.
harissa soak chilli in small heatproof bowl of boiling water 1 hour. Drain; reserve ¼ cup soaking liquid. Dry-fry spices in small heated frying pan until fragrant. Blend or process spices with chilli, reserved liquid, garlic and paste until smooth; transfer to small bowl, stir in rind and juice.
preparation time 35 minutes (plus standing time)
cooking time 2 hours **serves** 4
nutritional count per serving 37.5g total fat (10.7g saturated fat); 2717kJ (650 cal); 27.9g carbohydrate; 46.1g protein; 8.3g fibre

Tandoori wings

16 small chicken wings (1.3kg)
½ cup (150g) tandoori paste
½ cup (140g) yogurt
1 medium brown onion (150g), grated

1 Preheat oven to 220°C/200°C fan-forced.
2 Cut wings into three pieces at joints; discard tips. Combine chicken and remaining ingredients in large bowl. Cover; refrigerate 3 hours or overnight.
3 Place chicken, in single layer, on oiled wire rack set inside large shallow baking dish. Roast, uncovered, about 30 minutes or until chicken is well browned and cooked through.
4 Serve wings with lime wedges, if desired.

preparation time 10 minutes (plus refrigeration time)
cooking time 30 minutes **makes** 32
nutritional count per wing 3.0g total fat (0.7g saturated fat);
234kJ (56 cal); 0.8g carbohydrate; 6.4g protein; 0.5g fibre

Lebanese-spiced drumsticks with baba ghanoush

8 chicken drumsticks (1.2kg)
2 teaspoons ground allspice
1 teaspoon ground black pepper
1 teaspoon ground cumin
2 tablespoons olive oil
4 large pittas
baba ghanoush
2 medium eggplants (600g)
1 clove garlic, crushed
1 tablespoon tahini
¼ cup (60ml) lemon juice
2 tablespoons olive oil

1 Preheat oven to 200°C/180°C fan-forced.
2 Make baba ghanoush.
3 Meanwhile, combine drumsticks, spices and oil in large bowl.
4 Place drumsticks on oiled wire rack over baking dish. Roast, uncovered, about 50 minutes or until chicken is cooked through, turning occasionally.
5 Serve drumsticks with baba ghanoush and pitta and, if desired, lemon wedges and fresh parsley.
baba ghanoush pierce eggplants all over with fork; place on oiled oven tray. Roast, uncovered, about 40 minutes or until eggplant is soft, turning occasionally. Stand 10 minutes. Peel eggplant, discard skin; drain eggplant in colander 10 minutes. Blend or process eggplant with garlic, tahini, juice and oil.

preparation time 20 minutes
cooking time 50 minutes (plus standing time) **serves** 4
nutritional count per serving 44.4g total fat (9.5g saturated fat); 3164kJ (757 cal); 43.6g carbohydrate; 43.2g protein; 6.2g fibre

Roast chicken

1.5kg whole chicken
1 bunch fresh coriander (about 100g), roots intact
4 fresh kaffir lime leaves, torn
2 x 10cm sticks fresh lemon grass (40g), chopped coarsely
2 kaffir limes, quartered
cooking-oil spray
1 teaspoon sea salt flakes

1 Preheat oven to 200°C/180°C fan-forced.
2 Wash cavity of chicken under cold water; pat dry with absorbent paper.
3 Wash coriander under cold water, removing any dirt clinging to roots. Chop coriander roots, stems and leaves; place all of the coriander, lime leaves, lemon grass and 4 of the lime quarters inside cavity of chicken.
4 Tuck wings under chicken; trim skin around chicken neck, secure to underside of chicken with toothpicks. Tie legs together loosely using kitchen string.
5 Place chicken, breast-side up, on oiled wire rack inside large baking dish. Spray chicken with cooking-oil spray; sprinkle with salt.
6 Pour enough water into baking dish to come up to 1cm. Roast chicken, uncovered, for 1½ hours; cover loosely with foil after an hour if chicken starts to overbrown.
7 Remove and discard toothpicks, kitchen string and cavity filling. Serve chicken, carved or cut into pieces, with remaining lime quarters.

preparation time 30 minutes **cooking time** 1 hour 30 minutes
serves 4
nutritional count per serving 30.9g total fat (9.5g saturated fat); 1802kJ (431 cal); 0.6g carbohydrate; 38.0g protein; 0.6g fibre

Oven-baked drumsticks with soy bean salad

½ cup (100g) dried soy beans
8 chicken drumsticks (1.2kg)
1 tablespoon olive oil
1 tablespoon finely grated lemon rind
1 tablespoon finely chopped fresh oregano
1 cup loosely packed fresh flat-leaf parsley leaves
½ cup loosely packed fresh basil leaves
½ cup loosely packed fresh oregano leaves
½ small red onion (50g), sliced thinly
2 tablespoons lemon juice
1 clove garlic, crushed
sun-dried tomato coulis
1 medium brown onion (150g), chopped finely
4 medium tomatoes (600g), chopped coarsely
½ cup (140g) tomato paste
¼ cup drained sun-dried tomatoes in oil, chopped finely

1 Cover beans with cold water in medium bowl; stand overnight. Drain, rinse under cold water; drain. Place beans in medium saucepan of boiling water; return to the boil. Reduce heat; simmer, uncovered, 30 minutes or until beans are almost tender. Drain. Cool.
2 Preheat oven to 200°C/180°C fan-forced.
3 Meanwhile, remove and discard skin from drumsticks. Combine drumsticks with oil, rind and chopped oregano in large bowl. Place drumsticks, in single layer, in oiled shallow baking dish; roast, covered with foil, turning half-way through cooking, about 50 minutes or until cooked through.
4 Meanwhile, make sun-dried tomato coulis.
5 Combine beans in medium bowl with remaining herbs, onion, juice and garlic. Serve salad with chicken, topped with coulis.
sun-dried tomato coulis cook onion, tomato and paste in heated oiled medium saucepan, covered, about 20 minutes. Blend or process until smooth. Push mixture through sieve into medium bowl; discard solids. Stir in sun-dried tomato.
preparation time 25 minutes (plus standing time)
cooking time 50 minutes (plus cooling time) **serves** 4
nutritional count per serving 22.3g total fat (4.9g saturated fat); 2002kJ (479 cal); 14.7g carbohydrate; 48.1g protein; 11.3g fibre

Mediterranean chicken with burghul salad

1.6kg whole chicken
4 long red dutch chillies, chopped finely
4 cloves garlic, crushed
1 tablespoon ground cumin
1 tablespoon ground coriander
1 tablespoon finely grated lemon rind
1 tablespoon lemon juice
1 tablespoon olive oil
1 medium lemon (140g), cut into 8 wedges
burghul salad
½ cup (80g) burghul
2 medium tomatoes (380g), chopped finely
1 small red onion (100g), chopped finely
1 cup coarsely chopped fresh flat-leaf parsley
½ cup coarsely chopped fresh mint
½ cup coarsely chopped fresh coriander
¼ cup (60ml) lemon juice

1 Preheat oven to 180°C/160°C fan-forced.
2 Wash chicken under cold water; pat dry with absorbent paper. Using kitchen scissors, cut along both sides of backbone of chicken; discard backbone. Place chicken, skin-side up, on board; using heel of hand, press down on breastbone to flatten. Insert metal skewer through thigh and opposite wing to keep chicken flat. Repeat with other thigh and wing.
3 Combine chilli, garlic, spices, rind, juice and oil in small bowl. Using spatula or back of metal spoon, spread chilli mixture all over chicken.
4 Place chicken and lemon on oiled wire rack over baking dish; roast, uncovered, 1¼ hours or until browned and chicken is cooked through. Remove skewers.
5 Meanwhile, make burghul salad. Serve salad with chicken.
burghul salad soak burghul in small bowl of water 15 minutes; drain. Rinse under cold water, drain; squeeze to remove excess moisture. Combine burghul in medium bowl with remaining ingredients.
preparation time 30 minutes **cooking time** 1 hour 15 minutes
serves 4
nutritional count per serving 37.4g total fat (10.8g saturated fat); 2483kJ (594 cal); 16.9g carbohydrate; 44.5g protein; 7.2g fibre

Roasted spatchcock with dill and walnut pesto

⅓ cup firmly packed fresh flat-leaf parsley leaves
½ cup firmly packed fresh dill sprigs
½ cup (50g) roasted walnuts, chopped coarsely
¼ cup (20g) finely grated parmesan cheese
¼ cup (60ml) lemon juice
¼ cup (60ml) olive oil
4 x 500g spatchcocks
2 medium lemons (280g), quartered

risoni salad
1 cup (220g) risoni
6 slices pancetta (90g), chopped finely
⅓ cup (50g) roasted pine nuts
¼ cup finely chopped fresh basil
¼ cup finely chopped fresh flat-leaf parsley
2 tablespoons olive oil
1 tablespoon red wine vinegar

1 Preheat oven to 180°C/160°C fan-forced.
2 Blend or process herbs, nuts, cheese and juice until combined. With motor operating, gradually add oil in thin, steady stream until pesto thickens slightly. Reserve 1 tablespoon of pesto for risoni salad.
3 Wash spatchcocks under cold water. Discard necks; pat dry inside and out with absorbent paper. Loosen spatchcock skin; rub remaining pesto between skin and flesh and over outside of spatchcocks. Place 2 lemon quarters in cavity of each spatchcock.
4 Place spatchcocks on oiled wire rack over baking dish; roast, uncovered, 45 minutes or until cooked through. Remove from dish; discard pan juices.
5 Meanwhile, make risoni salad.
6 Serve spatchcocks, halved lengthways, on salad.
risoni salad cook pasta in large saucepan of boiling water, uncovered, until just tender; drain. Cook pancetta in heated oiled small frying pan, stirring, 5 minutes or until crisp. Place pasta and pancetta in large bowl with nuts, herbs, oil, vinegar and reserved pesto; toss gently to combine.

preparation time 55 minutes **cooking time** 45 minutes **serves** 4
nutritional count per serving 85.1g total fat (18.9g saturated fat); 5029kJ (1203 cal); 40.3g carbohydrate; 65.5g protein; 5.5g fibre

Italian roasted quail with braised vegetables

8 quails (1.3kg)
8 slices prosciutto (120g)
20g butter
½ cup (125ml) dry white wine
2 baby fennel bulbs (260g), trimmed, sliced thinly
4 cloves garlic, unpeeled
1 large red capsicum (350g), sliced thinly
2 medium zucchini (240g), halved lengthways, sliced thickly
½ cup (125ml) chicken stock
1 medium lemon (140g), cut into eight wedges
¼ cup (60ml) cream
1 tablespoon fresh oregano leaves

1 Preheat oven to 200°C/180°C fan-forced.
2 Discard necks from quails. Wash quails under cold water; pat dry inside and out with absorbent paper. Tuck legs along body; wrap tightly with prosciutto to hold legs in place.
3 Heat butter in large flameproof baking dish; cook quails, in batches, until browned all over.
4 Place wine in same dish; bring to the boil. Reduce heat; simmer, uncovered, until wine has reduced to 1 tablespoon. Add fennel, garlic, capsicum, zucchini and stock; return to the boil. Place quails on top of vegetables; roast, uncovered, in oven 20 minutes. Add lemon to dish; roast, uncovered, further 10 minutes or until quails are cooked through.
5 Remove quails and garlic from dish. When cool enough to handle, squeeze garlic from skins into dish; stir in cream and oregano.
6 Serve quails on vegetables.

preparation time 15 minutes **cooking time** 45 minutes **serves** 4
nutritional count per serving 30.8g total fat (12.4g saturated fat);
2052kJ (491 cal); 6.9g carbohydrate; 39.1g protein; 4.2g fibre

Slow-roasted seasoned turkey

4.5kg whole turkey
100g butter, melted
1 cup (250ml) salt-reduced chicken stock
⅓ cup (50g) plain flour
¼ cup (60ml) dry sherry
3 cups (750ml) salt-reduced chicken stock, extra
bacon seasoning
60g butter
1 large leek (500g), sliced thinly
4 rashers rindless bacon (260g), chopped coarsely
2 trimmed celery stalks (200g), chopped finely
1 tablespoon coarsely chopped fresh sage
4 cups (280g) coarse stale white breadcrumbs
1 egg, beaten lightly
¼ cup (40g) pine nuts, roasted
1 cup coarsely chopped fresh flat-leaf parsley

1 Make bacon seasoning. Preheat oven to 150°C/130°C fan-forced.
2 Discard neck from turkey. Rinse turkey under water; dry inside and out.
Fill neck cavity with seasoning; secure skin over opening with toothpicks.
Fill large cavity with seasoning; tie legs together, tuck wings under turkey.
3 Place turkey on oiled wired rack in baking dish. Dip 50cm square piece
muslin in butter, drape over turkey. Add stock to dish; cover with foil.
Roast 4 hours.
4 Remove foil and muslin, brush turkey with pan juices. Increase oven
temperature to 200°C/180°C fan-forced; roast further 45 minutes or
until browned. Remove turkey; cover with foil, stand 20 minutes. Remove
and discard toothpicks.
5 Drain pan juices into a jug; skim and reserve ¼ cup (60ml) of fat from
the surface. Stir reserved fat and flour in same baking dish, over heat,
until well browned. Gradually stir in sherry, extra stock and strained pan
juices; cook, stirring, until gravy boils and thickens.
6 Serve turkey with strained gravy and vegetables, if desired.
bacon seasoning heat butter in large frying pan; cook leek, bacon,
celery and sage, stirring, until leek softens. Combine leek mixture with
breadcrumbs, egg, pine nuts and parsley in medium bowl.
preparation time 25 minutes
cooking time 4 hours 45 minutes (plus standing time) **serves** 8
nutritional count per serving 62.5g total fat (23.9g saturated fat);
4167kJ (997 cal); 30.7g carbohydrate; 75.4g protein; 3.8g fibre

Garlic roasted duck

A duck wing portion consists of the wing and part of the breast.

2 tablespoons fish sauce
4 cloves garlic, crushed
1 cup (250ml) red wine vinegar
1 large brown onion (200g), chopped coarsely
2 teaspoons juniper berries, bruised
2 teaspoons fennel seeds
4 duck wing portions (1.5kg)
2 tablespoons yogurt

1 Combine fish sauce, garlic, vinegar, onion, berries and seeds in medium bowl. Place duck in single layer in shallow dish; pour over vinegar mixture. Cover; refrigerate 3 hours or overnight.
2 Preheat oven to 180°C/160°C fan-forced.
3 Remove duck from marinade; reserve marinade. Place duck, skin-side up, on oiled wire rack over baking dish; roast, uncovered, 45 minutes or until tender.
4 Place reserved marinade in small saucepan; simmer, uncovered, about 5 minutes or until slightly thickened, strain. Stir yogurt into sauce; serve with duck.

preparation time 15 minutes (plus refrigeration time)
cooking time 45 minutes **serves** 4
nutritional count per serving 79.2g total fat (23.9g saturated fat); 3507kJ (839 cal); 3.8g carbohydrate; 29.8g protein; 1.3g fibre

Mexican chicken with black bean and barley salad

½ cup (100g) dried black beans
2 cups (500ml) chicken stock
1 litre (4 cups) water
¾ cup (165g) pearl barley
4 x 170g single chicken breast fillets
35g packet taco seasoning mix
⅓ cup (80ml) chicken stock, extra
1 large red capsicum (350g), chopped finely
1 clove garlic, crushed
¼ cup (60ml) lime juice
2 teaspoons olive oil
½ cup loosely packed fresh coriander leaves

1 Preheat oven to 200°C/180°C fan-forced.
2 Combine beans with half of the stock and half of the water in medium saucepan; bring to the boil. Reduce heat; simmer, uncovered, 45 minutes or until tender, drain. Rinse under cold water; drain.
3 Meanwhile, combine barley with remaining stock and remaining water in medium saucepan; bring to the boil. Reduce heat; simmer, uncovered, until just tender; drain. Rinse under cold water; drain.
4 Place chicken in medium bowl; combine with blended seasoning and extra stock.
5 Drain chicken; reserve marinade. Place chicken, in single layer, on oiled wire rack in large shallow baking dish; roast, uncovered, about 30 minutes or until cooked through, brushing with reserved marinade halfway through cooking time. Cover; stand 5 minutes then slice thickly.
6 Place beans and barley in large bowl with remaining ingredients; toss gently to combine. Divide salad among serving plates; top with chicken.

preparation time 15 minutes
cooking time 45 minutes (plus standing time) **serves** 4
nutritional count per serving 13.4g total fat (2.7g saturated fat); 2086kJ (499 cal); 35.0g carbohydrate; 53.4g protein; 11.7g fibre

Glazed turkey with orange stuffing

4.5kg turkey
2 medium oranges (480g), unpeeled, chopped coarsely
1 cup (250ml) water
2 cups (500ml) chicken stock
½ cup (125ml) bourbon
50g butter, melted
½ cup (175g) honey
2 tablespoons orange juice
2 tablespoons plain flour
orange stuffing
20g butter
1 large brown onion (200g), chopped finely
4 cups (280g) stale breadcrumbs
1 cup (120g) coarsely chopped toasted pecans
1 tablespoon finely grated orange rind
2 tablespoons orange juice
½ cup (125ml) water
40g butter, melted
2 eggs, beaten lightly

1 Preheat oven to 180°C/160°C fan-forced.
2 Discard neck from turkey. Rinse turkey under cold water; pat dry inside and out with absorbent paper. Tuck wings under turkey; fill large cavity with orange, tie legs together with kitchen string.
3 Place the water, stock and bourbon into large baking dish; place turkey on oiled wire rack over dish. Brush turkey with butter; cover with oiled foil. Roast 2 hours 10 minutes. Brush with half of the combined honey and juice. Roast, uncovered, 50 minutes or until cooked through, brushing often with remaining honey mixture. Remove turkey from dish; cover, stand 20 minutes.
4 Meanwhile, make orange stuffing.
5 Strain pan juices into large jug. Skim off 2 tablespoons of the oil; return oil to dish. Add flour; cook, stirring, until browned. Add juices; cook, stirring, until gravy boils and thickens. Strain gravy; serve with turkey.
orange stuffing melt butter in medium frying pan; cook onion, stirring, until soft. Combine onion in medium bowl with remaining ingredients. Roll rounded tablespoons into balls; place on oiled tray. Roast 20 minutes.
preparation time 30 minutes **cooking time** 3 hours **serves** 8
nutritional count per serving 60.7g total fat (19.5g saturated fat); 4619kJ (1105 cal); 58.8g carbohydrate; 69.7g protein; 4.4g fibre

Roast chicken and beetroot with pesto butter

1.6kg whole chicken
1 medium brown onion (150g), quartered
1 bulb garlic, separated into cloves
cooking-oil spray
1 teaspoon salt
8 small fresh beetroot (800g)
pesto butter
125g butter, softened
1 tablespoon lemon juice
⅓ cup coarsely chopped fresh basil
2 tablespoons pine nuts, roasted
2 cloves garlic, crushed
2 tablespoons grated parmesan cheese

1 Make pesto butter.
2 Preheat oven to 180°C/160°C fan-forced.
3 Wash the cavity of the chicken under cold water; pat dry with absorbent paper. Tuck wings under chicken. Loosen skin of the chicken by sliding fingers carefully between skin and meat. Spread half of the pesto butter under skin; spread mixture evenly over breast by pressing with fingers. Place onion and two of the garlic cloves inside chicken cavity. Tie legs of chicken together with kitchen string.
4 Place chicken, breast-side up, on oiled wire rack in large baking dish; spray chicken with oil spray, sprinkle with salt. Roast, uncovered, about 45 minutes. Add unpeeled beetroot to dish; roast, uncovered, further 15 minutes. Add remaining unpeeled garlic cloves to dish; roast further 30 minutes or until chicken and beetroot are cooked. Cover loosely with foil if chicken starts to over-brown.
5 Cover chicken to keep warm; stand 10 minutes. Peel beetroot.
6 Serve chicken with beetroot, garlic and remaining pesto butter.
pesto butter process ingredients until almost smooth.

preparation time 25 minutes
cooking time 1 hour 30 minutes (plus standing time) **serves** 4
nutritional count per serving 65.3g total fat (28.0g saturated fat); 3595kJ (860 cal); 18.8g carbohydrate; 47.0g protein; 8.4g fibre

Marinated chilli spatchcock

8 fresh medium red chillies
8 cloves garlic, peeled
2 small brown onions (200g), chopped finely
⅓ cup (80ml) red wine vinegar
1 tablespoon ground cumin
2 tablespoons olive oil
4 medium ripe tomatoes (750g), quartered
4 x 500g spatchcocks

1 Process chillies, garlic, onion, vinegar and cumin until almost smooth.
2 Heat oil in medium frying pan, add chilli mixture; bring to the boil, stirring.
3 Process tomatoes until smooth, add to pan; cook, stirring, until mixture boils. Reduce heat; simmer, uncovered, stirring, about 20 minutes or until thickened. Cool. Refrigerate half of the mixture.
4 Cut spatchcocks in half, remove neck and backbone. Rub remaining chilli mixture over spatchcocks. Cover; refrigerate 3 hours or overnight.
5 Preheat oven to 220°C/200°C fan-forced.
6 Place spatchcocks, skin-side up, on oiled wire rack in shallow baking dish; sprinkle with salt. Roast, uncovered, 30 minutes or until tender.
7 Serve reserved chilli mixture at room temperature, with spatchcock.

preparation time 20 minutes (plus refrigeration time)
cooking time 1 hour (plus cooling time) **serves** 8
nutritional count per serving 24.5g total fat (6.8g saturated fat); 1425kJ (341 cal); 3.6g carbohydrate; 26.0g protein; 2.0g fibre

Salt and pepper duck with shallots and cucumber

2kg duck
1 tablespoon finely ground sichuan peppercorns
2 teaspoons sea salt
1 tablespoon peanut oil
20g butter
16 shallots (400g)
2 lebanese cucumbers (260g), sliced thickly
1 tablespoon oyster sauce
½ cup (125ml) chicken stock
¼ cup coarsely chopped fresh coriander

1 Preheat oven to 180°C/160°C fan-forced.
2 Place duck, breast-side up, on oiled wire rack in baking dish; rub combined pepper and salt into duck breast. Roast, uncovered, 1½ hours. Remove duck from oven; increase oven temperature to 240°C/220°C fan-forced.
3 Using metal skewer or fork, prick duck skin all over. Turn duck breast-side down; roast, uncovered, 15 minutes. Turn duck breast-side up; roast, uncovered, 20 minutes or until browned and cooked through.
4 Meanwhile, heat oil and butter in large frying pan; cook shallots, stirring, until softened. Add cucumber; cook, stirring, 2 minutes. Stir in combined sauce and stock; bring to the boil. Remove from heat; stir in coriander.
5 Cut duck into pieces, serve on shallot and cucumber mixture; sprinkle with fresh coriander, if desired.

preparation time 10 minutes **cooking time** 2 hours 5 minutes
serves 4
nutritional count per serving 114.2g total fat (35.2g saturated fat); 4995kJ (1195 cal); 5.6g carbohydrate; 39.2g protein; 1.7g fibre
tip use zucchini instead of lebanese cucumber, if you prefer.

Roast chicken with fennel and garlic

1.8kg whole chicken
2 medium lemons (280g)
8 cloves garlic
50g butter, softened
1 teaspoon grated lemon rind
1 tablespoon chopped fresh lemon thyme
¼ teaspoon salt
2 medium carrots (240g)
2 small fennel bulbs (400g), quartered
4 trimmed celery stalks (400g), chopped coarsely
¼ cup (60ml) chicken stock

1 Preheat oven to 220°C/200°C fan-forced. Wash chicken, remove excess fat from inside neck cavity and remove giblets or neck if necessary. Pat dry with absorbent paper.
2 Cut lemons into quarters. Place two lemon quarters and two peeled cloves of garlic inside cavity of chicken.
3 Combine butter, two chopped cloves of peeled garlic, rind, thyme and salt in small bowl; rub all over chicken. Place chicken in large oiled baking dish; roast 20 minutes.
4 Cut carrots in half lengthways then in half crossways. Place carrots with fennel, celery, remaining lemon quarters, remaining unpeeled garlic and stock around chicken in dish. Roast further 50 minutes or until chicken is cooked through. Remove chicken from dish; cover with foil and stand 10 minutes.
5 Increase oven temperature to 240°C/220°C fan-forced. Roast vegetables further 15 minutes or until browned.
6 Serve chicken with vegetables and pan juices.

preparation time 15 minutes
cooking time 1 hour 25 minutes (plus standing time) **serves** 4
nutritional count per serving 46.9g total fat (18.1g saturated fat); 2709kJ (648 cal); 7.1g carbohydrate; 42.2g protein; 6.6g fibre

Chicken with garlic potatoes and rosemary

8 x 200g chicken thigh cutlets (chicken chops)
800g baby new potatoes, halved
30g butter, melted
2 rashers rindless bacon (130g), chopped coarsely
2 cloves garlic, sliced thinly
2 tablespoons fresh rosemary leaves
¼ cup (30g) green olives

1 Preheat oven to 240°C/220°C fan-forced. Cut two deep slashes through skin and flesh of the chicken to the bone.
2 Place chicken and potato in large, heavy-based flameproof baking dish. Brush with butter; roast, uncovered, 30 minutes.
3 Add bacon, garlic and rosemary to dish; roast, uncovered, further 10 minutes or until browned. Add olives.
4 Serve chicken and potato with a mixed salad and lemon wedges, if desired.

preparation time 10 minutes **cooking time** 40 minutes **serves** 4
nutritional count per serving 50.8g total fat (18.8g saturated fat); 3377kJ (808 cal); 27.9g carbohydrate; 58.0g protein; 4.3g fibre

Roast turkey with forcemeat stuffing

4.5kg whole turkey
1 cup (250ml) water
80g butter, melted
¼ cup (35g) plain flour
3 cups (750ml) chicken stock
½ cup (125ml) dry white wine
forcemeat stuffing
40g butter
3 medium brown onions (450g), chopped finely
2 rashers rindless bacon (130g), chopped coarsely
1 cup (70g) stale breadcrumbs
2 tablespoons finely chopped fresh tarragon
½ cup coarsely chopped fresh flat-leaf parsley
½ cup (75g) coarsely chopped roasted pistachios
250g pork mince
250g chicken mince

1 Make forcemeat stuffing.
2 Preheat oven to 180°C/160°C fan-forced.
3 Discard neck from turkey. Rinse turkey under cold water; pat dry inside and out with absorbent paper. Fill neck cavity loosely with stuffing; secure skin over opening with toothpicks. Fill large cavity loosely with stuffing; tie legs together with kitchen string.
4 Place turkey on oiled wire rack in large shallow flameproof baking dish; pour the water into dish. Brush turkey all over with half of the butter; cover tightly with two layers of oiled foil. Roast 2 hours. Brush with remaining butter; roast, uncovered, further 45 minutes or until browned and cooked through. Remove turkey from dish; cover, stand 20 minutes.
5 Pour pan juices into large jug; skim 1 tablespoon of the fat from juice, return to same dish. Skim and discard remaining fat from juice. Add flour to dish; cook, stirring, until mixture bubbles and is well browned. Gradually stir in stock, wine and remaining juice; bring to the boil, stirring, until gravy boils and thickens. Strain gravy into same jug; serve with turkey.
forcemeat stuffing melt butter in medium frying pan; cook onion and bacon, stirring, until onion softens. Combine with remaining ingredients.
preparation time 40 minutes
cooking time 3 hours 10 minutes (plus standing time) **serves** 10
nutritional count per serving 47.5g total fat (17.2g saturated fat); 3102kJ (742 cal); 11.4g carbohydrate; 65.1g protein; 1.8g fibre

Chinese barbecued wings with fried rice

You need to cook 1½ cups (300g) white long-grain rice the day before making this recipe. Spread cooled cooked rice on a tray, cover; refrigerate overnight.

10 large chicken wings (1.2kg)
2 tablespoons honey
2 tablespoons soy sauce
2 fresh small red thai chillies, chopped finely
fried rice
1 tablespoon peanut oil
2 eggs, beaten lightly
4 rashers rindless bacon (260g), chopped coarsely
3 green onions, sliced thinly
½ cup (60g) frozen peas
½ cup (80g) frozen corn kernels
1 tablespoon soy sauce
3 cups cold cooked white long-grain rice

1 Preheat oven to 200°C/180°C fan-forced.
2 Cut wings into three pieces at joints; discard wing tips. Combine wings, honey, sauce and chilli in large bowl.
3 Place undrained wings, in single layer, on oiled wire rack in large shallow baking dish; reserve any marinade in bowl. Roast, uncovered, brushing wings with marinade occasionally, about 40 minutes or until browned and cooked through, turning halfway through cooking time.
4 Meanwhile, make fried rice.
5 Serve wings with fried rice.
fried rice heat half of the oil in wok; cook egg over medium heat, swirling wok to form thin omelette. Remove from pan; cool. Roll omelette, cut into thin slices. Heat remaining oil in same wok; stir-fry bacon until crisp. Add remaining ingredients and omelette slices; stir-fry until hot.

preparation time 15 minutes
cooking time 40 minutes (plus cooling time) **serves** 4
nutritional count per serving 23.1g total fat (6.9g saturated fat); 2876kJ (688 cal); 57.2g carbohydrate; 61.3g protein; 2.8g fibre

Moroccan chicken with couscous stuffing

1.6kg whole chicken
20g butter, melted
20 vine-ripened truss cherry tomatoes (400g)
1 tablespoon olive oil
couscous stuffing
1 teaspoon olive oil
1 medium brown onion (150g), chopped finely
1½ cups (375ml) chicken stock
¼ cup (60ml) olive oil
1 tablespoon finely grated lemon rind
¼ cup (60ml) lemon juice
1 cup (200g) couscous
½ cup (70g) roasted slivered almonds
1 cup (140g) seeded dried dates, chopped finely
1 teaspoon ground cinnamon
1 teaspoon smoked paprika
1 egg, beaten lightly

1 Make couscous stuffing.
2 Preheat oven to 200°C/180°C fan-forced.
3 Wash chicken under cold water; pat dry inside and out with absorbent paper. Fill large cavity loosely with couscous stuffing; tie legs together with kitchen string. Place chicken on oiled wire rack over large baking dish; half fill with water. Brush chicken all over with butter; roast, uncovered, 15 minutes. Reduce oven temperature to 180°C/160°C fan-forced; roast, uncovered, further 1½ hours or until cooked through. Remove chicken from rack; cover, stand 20 minutes.
4 Meanwhile, place tomatoes on oven tray; drizzle with oil. Roast, uncovered, 20 minutes or until softened and browned. Serve with chicken.
couscous stuffing heat oil in small frying pan; cook onion, stirring, until soft. Combine stock, extra oil, rind and juice in medium saucepan; bring to the boil. Remove from heat. Add couscous, cover; stand 5 minutes or until stock is absorbed, fluffing with fork occasionally. Stir in onion, nuts, dates, spices and egg.

preparation time 30 minutes **cooking time** 2 hours (plus standing time)
serves 4
nutritional count per serving 67.5g total fat (16.7g saturated fat); 4631kJ (1108 cal); 67.8g carbohydrate; 54.9g protein; 7.2g fibre

Honey ginger baked chicken

10cm piece fresh ginger (50g), sliced thinly
1 medium lemon (140g)
¼ cup (55g) firmly packed brown sugar
⅓ cup (120g) honey
¼ cup (60ml) water
2 cloves garlic, crushed
1 fresh large green chilli, chopped, optional
4 x 200g chicken thigh cutlets
4 x 150g chicken drumsticks
3 green onions, sliced thinly

1 Cut ginger slices into thin strips. Remove rind thinly from lemon using a zester, or peel rind with a vegetable peeler, avoiding the white pith; cut rind into thin strips.
2 Stir sugar, honey and the water in medium saucepan over medium heat until sugar is dissolved; bring to the boil. Add ginger; simmer, stirring, 5 minutes or until ginger is tender. Transfer to large heatproof bowl; stir in garlic, chilli and rind.
3 Cut deep slashes through the thick part of the chicken flesh at 2cm intervals; combine with honey ginger mixture. Cover; refrigerate 3 hours or overnight, turning chicken occasionally.
4 Preheat oven to 180°C/160°C fan-forced. Place chicken mixture, in single layer, in medium baking dish. Roast, uncovered, about 40 minutes or until chicken is browned and cooked through.
5 Top chicken with green onions and serve with steamed rice, if desired.

preparation time 20 minutes (plus refrigeration time)
cooking time 45 minutes **serves** 4
nutritional count per serving 30.6g total fat (9.8g saturated fat); 2491kJ (596 cal); 39.1g carbohydrate; 40.6g protein; 0.9g fibre

Roast chicken with red onions, garlic and cherries

1.8kg whole chicken
3 sprigs fresh thyme
½ lemon
10 cloves garlic
30g butter, softened
3 medium red onions (500g), cut into wedges
2 tablespoons olive oil
1½ cups (225g) fresh cherries

1 Preheat oven to 180°C/160°C fan-forced.
2 Wash the cavity of the chicken under cold water; pat dry with absorbent paper. Insert two of the thyme sprigs, lemon and two of the garlic cloves into the cavity. Tuck wings under chicken, tie chicken legs together with kitchen string.
3 Place chicken, breast-side up, on oiled wire rack in small baking dish. Rub chicken all over with butter; roast, uncovered, 20 minutes.
4 Combine onion, remaining garlic and oil in medium baking dish. Roast onion mixture alongside chicken further 50 minutes.
5 Add cherries to onion mixture, toss gently to combine; sprinkle remaining thyme over chicken. Roast chicken and cherry mixture further 10 minutes or until chicken is tender and cherries are hot.

preparation time 20 minutes **cooking time** 1 hour 20 minutes
serves 4
nutritional count per serving 51.8g total fat (16.7g saturated fat); 2955kJ (707 cal); 11.8g carbohydrate; 47.6g protein; 3.8g fibre

Chorizo-stuffed roast chicken

20g butter
1 medium brown onion (150g), chopped finely
1 chorizo sausage (170g), diced into 1cm pieces
1½ cups (110g) stale breadcrumbs
½ cup (100g) ricotta cheese
1 egg
¼ cup finely chopped fresh flat-leaf parsley
¼ cup (35g) roasted slivered almonds
1.6kg whole chicken
2 medium lemons (280g), cut into wedges
spinach and red onion salad
150g baby spinach leaves
1 small red onion (100g), sliced thinly
1 tablespoon red wine vinegar
2 tablespoons olive oil

1 Melt half of the butter in medium frying pan; cook onion and chorizo, stirring, until onion softens. Cool 10 minutes. Combine chorizo mixture in medium bowl with breadcrumbs, cheese, egg, parsley and nuts.
2 Preheat oven to 200°C/180°C fan-forced.
3 Wash chicken under cold water; pat dry inside and out with absorbent paper. Tuck wing tips under chicken. Trim skin around neck; secure neck flap to underside of chicken with skewers.
4 Fill cavity with chorizo mixture, fold over skin to enclose stuffing; secure with toothpicks. Tie legs together with kitchen string. Place chicken and lemon in medium baking dish; rub chicken all over with remaining butter. Roast, uncovered, about 1½ hours or until chicken is cooked through, basting occasionally with pan juices. Remove and discard toothpicks.
5 Meanwhile, place ingredients for spinach and red onion salad in large bowl; toss gently to combine.
6 Serve chicken with stuffing, lemon and salad.

preparation time 25 minutes
cooking time 1 hour 35 minutes (plus cooling time) **serves** 4
nutritional count per serving 68.4g total fat (21.4g saturated fat); 4042kJ (967 cal); 24.4g carbohydrate; 60.3g protein; 5.8g fibre

Slow-roasted duck with sour cherry, apple and walnut salad

680g jar morello cherries
½ cup (125ml) chicken stock
½ cup (125ml) port
1 cinnamon stick
3 whole cloves
1 clove garlic, crushed
4 duck marylands (1.2kg), excess fat removed
2 small green apples (260g)
1 cup (100g) roasted walnuts, chopped coarsely
3 green onions, sliced thinly
1 cup firmly packed fresh flat-leaf parsley leaves
2 tablespoons olive oil
1 tablespoon lemon juice

1 Preheat oven to 160°C/140°C fan-forced.
2 Strain cherries over small bowl. Combine cherry juice with stock, port, cinnamon, cloves and garlic in large baking dish. Place duck on oiled wire rack over dish; cover tightly with oiled foil. Roast, covered, about 2 hours or until duck meat is tender.
3 Strain pan liquid into large jug; skim and discard fat. Reserve cherry sauce for serving.
4 Cut apples into thin slices; cut slices into matchstick-sized pieces. Place apple and seeded cherries in large bowl with nuts, onion, parsley, oil and lemon juice; toss gently to combine.
5 Serve duck with salad and reheated cherry sauce.

preparation time 40 minutes **cooking time** 2 hours **serves** 4
nutritional count per serving 30.5g total fat (3.6g saturated fat); 1977kJ (473 cal); 25.1g carbohydrate; 15.0g protein; 5.0g fibre
tip slice apples just before serving to prevent discolouration.

Roast turkey with sausage seasoning

4kg whole turkey
2 tablespoons olive oil
3 cups (750ml) chicken stock
40g butter
¼ cup (35g) plain flour
¼ cup (60ml) sweet sherry
sausage seasoning
1 tablespoon olive oil
1 small brown onion (80g), chopped finely
2 trimmed celery stalks (200g), chopped finely
2 rashers rindless bacon (130g), chopped finely
250g Italian sausages
4 cups (280g) stale breadcrumbs
2 teaspoons finely grated lemon rind
2 teaspoons lemon juice
2 tablespoons finely chopped fresh flat-leaf parsley
1 egg, beaten lightly

1 Make sausage seasoning. Preheat oven to 180°C/160°C fan-forced.
2 Discard neck from turkey. Rinse turkey under cold running water; pat dry inside and out with absorbent paper. Fill neck cavity loosely with seasoning, secure skin over opening with toothpicks; fill large cavity loosely with seasoning. Tie legs with kitchen string; tuck wings under turkey.
3 Place turkey on oiled wire rack in large flameproof baking dish. Brush turkey with oil; add 1 cup of the stock to dish. Cover with two layers of oiled foil; roast 2½ hours. Uncover; brush with pan juices. Roast, uncovered, 30 minutes or until browned all over and cooked through. Remove turkey from dish, cover; stand 20 minutes. Remove and discard toothpicks.
4 Drain pan juices from dish into large jug; skim and discard fat.
5 Melt butter in same dish over heat; cook flour, stirring, until mixture bubbles and thickens. Gradually add sherry, remaining stock and reserved pan juices; stir until it boils and thickens. Strain into same jug to serve.
sausage seasoning heat oil in medium frying pan; cook onion, celery and bacon, stirring, until onion softens. Squeeze sausage meat into large bowl; discard casings. Stir in onion mixture and remaining ingredients.
preparation time 20 minutes
cooking time 3 hours (plus standing time) **serves** 8
nutritional count per serving 56.5g total fat (17.9g saturated fat); 3816kJ (913 cal); 29.4g carbohydrate; 69.7g protein; 2.3g fibre

beef+veal

Veal rack with roasted mushroom sauce

1kg veal rack
¼ cup (60ml) olive oil
1kg baby new potatoes
300g button mushrooms
150g shimeji or oyster mushrooms
2 cloves garlic, sliced
2 tablespoons grated parmesan cheese
2 tablespoons plain flour
1½ cups (375ml) chicken stock
⅓ cup (80ml) cream
2 tablespoons chopped fresh flat-leaf parsley

1 Preheat oven to 200°C/180°C fan-forced.
2 Place veal on oiled wire rack in shallow flameproof medium baking dish. Rub veal with 1 tablespoon of the oil, sprinkle with sea salt flakes and freshly ground black pepper; roast for 10 minutes.
3 Place potatoes in small baking dish; roast potatoes alongside veal for further 30 minutes or until veal is cooked as desired, brushing with any pan juices. Remove veal from dish; cover to keep warm.
4 Combine mushrooms, garlic and remaining oil in veal baking dish; roast mushroom mixture alongside potatoes for further 20 minutes or until potatoes are tender. Sprinkle potatoes with cheese, then roast a further 5 minutes or until cheese is melted.
5 Meanwhile, place mushroom mixture in baking dish over medium heat, add flour; cook, stirring, about 2 minutes or until bubbling. Gradually stir in stock and any veal pan juices; cook, stirring, until sauce boils and thickens. Stir in cream and parsley until heated through.
6 Cut the veal into cutlets, serve with mushroom sauce and potatoes.

preparation time 20 minutes **cooking time** 1 hour 5 minutes
serves 4
nutritional count per serving 29.0g total fat (10.0g saturated fat); 2792kJ (668 cal); 38.7g carbohydrate; 58.4g protein; 9.1g fibre

Roast beef with yorkshire puddings and red wine gravy

2 tablespoons wholegrain mustard
1 tablespoon port
1 ½ tablespoons worcestershire sauce
2kg piece boneless beef sirloin
1 ½ cups (375ml) water
1 cup (250ml) dry red wine
40g butter
2 tablespoons plain flour
1 ½ cups (375ml) beef stock
yorkshire puddings
1 cup (150g) plain flour
1 teaspoon salt
1 cup (250ml) milk
2 eggs

1 Preheat oven to 220°C/200°C fan-forced.
2 Rub combined mustard, port and 1 tablespoon of sauce all over beef. Place beef on oiled wire rack in flameproof baking dish; pour combined water and ½ cup (125ml) of the wine into dish. Roast, uncovered, 10 minutes. Reduce oven temperature to 180°C/160°C fan-forced; roast 45 minutes or until cooked as desired. Add water if pan juices evaporate.
3 Make batter for yorkshire puddings.
4 Transfer beef to a plate; cover to keep warm. Increase oven temperature to 240°C/220°C fan-forced. Drain pan juices into small heatproof bowl; freeze 10 minutes. Scrape solidified fat from top of pan juices; reserve pan juices. Divide 2 tablespoons of the fat (if necessary, use olive oil) among two 12-hole mini muffin pans. Preheat pans in oven 3 minutes; immediately divide batter among holes. Bake 15 minutes or until browned and risen.
5 Melt butter in same baking dish; cook flour, stirring, until mixture is well browned. Gradually stir in remaining wine then stock, remaining sauce and reserved pan juices; cook, stirring until gravy boils and thickens slightly. Strain into jug; serve with beef, yorkshire puddings and peas, if desired.
yorkshire puddings sift flour and salt into medium bowl. Whisk in combined milk and eggs until batter is smooth. Cover; stand 30 minutes.
preparation time 25 minutes **cooking time** 1 hour 15 minutes **serves** 6
nutritional count per serving 23.5g total fat (11.3g saturated fat); 2784kJ (666 cal); 24.8g carbohydrate; 79.7g protein; 1.4g fibre

Herbed beef fillet with horseradish cream sauce

1 tablespoon finely grated lemon rind
⅓ cup (80ml) lemon juice
1 teaspoon dried chilli flakes
3 cloves garlic, crushed
¼ cup coarsely chopped fresh flat-leaf parsley
¼ cup loosely packed fresh oregano leaves
¼ cup coarsely chopped fresh basil
¼ cup loosely packed fresh marjoram leaves
⅓ cup (80ml) olive oil
2kg piece beef tenderloin
horseradish cream sauce
1 tablespoon olive oil
2 cloves garlic, crushed
2 teaspoons plain flour
½ cup (125ml) dry white wine
½ cup (140g) horseradish cream
600ml cream

1 Preheat oven to 160°C/140°C fan-forced.
2 Combine rind, juice, chilli, garlic, herbs and oil in large bowl. Coat beef all over with herb mixture. Place beef on oiled wire rack in large shallow baking dish. Roast, uncovered, about 40 minutes or until cooked as desired. Cover beef; stand 10 minutes.
3 Meanwhile, make horseradish cream sauce.
4 Serve sliced beef with sauce and beans, if desired.
horseradish cream sauce heat oil in small frying pan; cook garlic and flour, stirring, until mixtures bubbles and browns lightly. Gradually stir in wine; bring to the boil, stirring. Reduce heat; simmer, uncovered, until liquid reduces by half. Stir in horseradish and cream; simmer, stirring, about 5 minutes or until sauce thickens slightly.

preparation time 15 minutes
cooking time 40 minutes (plus standing time) **serves** 8
nutritional count per serving 60.5g total fat (30.4g saturated fat); 3319kJ (794 cal); 5.7g carbohydrate; 55.2g protein; 0.8g fibre

Beef fillet with chermoulla

700g piece beef eye fillet
chermoulla
2 tablespoons olive oil
¼ cup coarsely chopped fresh flat-leaf parsley
2 tablespoons coarsely chopped fresh coriander
2 teaspoons grated lemon rind
1 tablespoon lemon juice
2 teaspoons sweet paprika
1 teaspoon ground cumin
1 teaspoon ground coriander
1 teaspoon salt

1 Preheat oven to 200°C/180°C fan-forced.
2 Combine ingredients for chermoulla in large bowl.
3 Tie beef with kitchen string at 2cm intervals to keep its shape. Coat beef all over with chermoulla.
4 Place beef on oiled wire rack in baking dish. Roast, uncovered, 30 minutes or until cooked as desired. Cover; stand 10 minutes. Remove string and slice.
5 Serve beef with lemon wedges, if desired.

preparation time 15 minutes
cooking time 30 minutes (plus standing time) **serves** 4
nutritional count per serving 19.4g total fat (5.7g saturated fat); 1359kJ (325 cal); 0.2g carbohydrate; 37.3g protein; 0.3g fibre
tip beef can be marinated for 2 hours, if preferred. It is best cooked close to serving.

Mustard-crusted rack of veal with kumara mash

2 tablespoons wholegrain mustard
3 green onions, chopped finely
2 cloves garlic, crushed
1 tablespoon finely chopped fresh rosemary
2 tablespoons olive oil
1kg veal rack (8 cutlets), trimmed
2 small kumara (500g), chopped coarsely
20g butter
⅓ cup (80ml) cream
1 large brown onion (200g), sliced thinly
400g mushrooms, sliced thinly
1 tablespoon plain flour
¼ cup (60ml) dry white wine
¾ cup (180ml) chicken stock
¼ cup coarsely chopped fresh flat-leaf parsley

1 Preheat oven to 200°C/180°C fan-forced.
2 Combine mustard, green onion, half of the garlic, rosemary and half of the oil in small jug. Place veal on oiled wire rack over large shallow flameproof baking dish; coat veal all over with mustard mixture. Roast, uncovered, about 30 minutes or until browned all over and cooked as desired. Cover to keep warm.
3 Meanwhile, boil, steam or microwave kumara until tender; drain. Mash kumara in large bowl with butter and half of the cream until smooth.
4 Heat remaining oil in same flameproof dish; cook brown onion and remaining garlic, stirring, until onion softens. Add mushrooms; cook, stirring, about 5 minutes or until just tender. Add flour; cook, stirring, until mixture bubbles and thickens. Gradually stir in wine and stock; stir until sauce boils and thickens. Add remaining cream and parsley; stir until heated through.
5 Serve veal with kumara mash and mushroom sauce.

preparation time 25 minutes **cooking time** 35 minutes **serves** 4
nutritional count per serving 27.4g total fat (11.2g saturated fat); 2370kJ (567 cal); 21.8g carbohydrate; 53.2g protein; 6.0g fibre

Corned beef with sticky redcurrant glaze

1.5kg piece beef corned silverside
2 bay leaves
¼ cup (60ml) malt vinegar
¼ cup (50g) firmly packed brown sugar
8 black peppercorns
8 cloves
1 medium brown onion (150g), chopped coarsely
1 trimmed celery stalk (100g), chopped coarsely
800g baby carrots
1 tablespoon olive oil
2 cloves garlic, crushed
1½ cups (375ml) chicken stock
sticky redcurrant glaze
¾ cup (180g) redcurrant jelly
¼ cup (60ml) port
1 tablespoon fresh rosemary leaves

1 Place beef, bay leaves, vinegar, sugar, peppercorns, cloves, onion and celery in large saucepan. Cover with cold water; bring to the boil. Reduce heat; simmer, uncovered, 1 hour. Remove beef from stock.
2 Preheat oven to 220°C/200°C fan-forced.
3 Make sticky redcurrant glaze.
4 Place beef in large flameproof baking dish; brush with half of the glaze. Add carrots to dish; drizzle with combined oil and garlic. Roast, uncovered, about 30 minutes or until browned all over and tender, brushing beef occasionally with remaining glaze. Remove beef and carrots from dish; cover to keep warm.
5 Add chicken stock to same baking dish; bring to the boil. Reduce heat; simmer, stirring, until sauce thickens slightly.
6 Serve beef and carrots topped with sauce.
sticky redcurrant glaze bring ingredients to the boil in small saucepan. Reduce heat; simmer, uncovered, 5 minutes or until glaze thickens slightly.

preparation time 15 minutes **cooking time** 2 hours **serves** 4
nutritional count per serving 15.7g total fat (5.3g saturated fat); 2805kJ (671 cal); 56.9g carbohydrate; 67.3g protein; 7.2g fibre
tip remaining beef stock in step 1 can be used as a base for soup; refrigerate until cold, then discard fat from the top before using.

Beef rib roast with roast vegetables

1.2kg beef standing rib roast
¼ cup (60ml) olive oil
2 teaspoons cracked black pepper
500g baby new potatoes
500g pumpkin, chopped coarsely
500g kumara, chopped coarsely
½ cup (125ml) brandy
1½ cups (375ml) beef stock
1 tablespoon cornflour
¼ cup (60ml) water
1 tablespoon finely chopped fresh chives

1 Preheat oven to 200°C/180°C fan-forced.
2 Brush beef with 1 tablespoon of the oil; sprinkle with pepper. Heat 1 tablespoon of the oil in large shallow flameproof baking dish; cook beef, uncovered, over high heat until browned all over. Place dish in oven; roast, uncovered, about 45 minutes or until cooked as desired.
3 Meanwhile, heat remaining oil in another large flameproof baking dish; cook potatoes, stirring, over high heat until browned lightly. Add pumpkin and kumara; roast, uncovered, in oven about 35 minutes or until vegetables are browned.
4 Place beef on vegetables, cover; return to oven to keep warm.
5 Drain pan juices from beef baking dish into medium saucepan, add brandy; bring to the boil. Stir in stock and blended cornflour and the water, stirring, until sauce boils and thickens slightly. Stir in chives; pour into medium heatproof jug.
6 Serve beef and vegetables with sauce.

preparation time 20 minutes **cooking time** 1 hour 30 minutes
serves 4
nutritional count per serving 30.5g total fat (9.2g saturated fat); 3219kJ (770 cal); 40.9g carbohydrate; 63.9g protein; 5.7g fibre

Veal loin with baked figs and port sauce

This cut of veal includes the tenderloin of veal, which is very pale in colour (almost white), is trimmed of any excess fat, and has a firm, velvety texture.

800g piece boneless loin of veal roast
¼ cup (60ml) balsamic vinegar
2 tablespoons olive oil
1 clove garlic, crushed
9 medium fresh figs (540g), halved
1 litre (4 cups) water
3 cups (750ml) milk
1½ cups (255g) polenta
40g butter
½ cup (125ml) cream
4 green onions, chopped finely
½ cup coarsely chopped fresh flat-leaf parsley
⅓ cup (80ml) port
1 cup (250ml) beef stock
1 tablespoon cornflour
¼ cup (60ml) water, extra

1 Place veal in large bowl with combined vinegar, oil and garlic; coat veal all over in marinade. Cover; refrigerate 3 hours or overnight.
2 Preheat oven to 200°C/180°C fan-forced.
3 Drain veal; discard marinade. Heat large flameproof baking dish; cook veal, uncovered, until browned all over. Roast, uncovered, in oven 30 minutes. Add fig halves; roast, uncovered, further 10 minutes or until figs are just tender.
4 Meanwhile, bring the water and milk to the boil in large saucepan. Stir polenta into liquid, stirring constantly. Reduce heat; simmer, stirring, about 20 minutes or until it thickens. Stir in butter, cream, onion and parsley.
5 Remove veal and figs from baking dish; cover to keep warm. Place dish with pan juices over high heat, add port; bring to the boil. Cook, stirring, 2 minutes. Add stock; bring to the boil, cook 3 minutes. Stir in blended cornflour and extra water, stirring, until sauce boils and thickens.
6 Serve veal on polenta, topped with figs and drizzled with sauce.
preparation time 10 minutes (plus refrigeration time)
cooking time 50 minutes **serves** 6
nutritional count per serving 28.7g total fat (14.3g saturated fat); 2625kJ (628 cal); 47.1g carbohydrate; 39.9g protein; 4.0g fibre

Roasted beef eye fillet with rösti and mushrooms

2 tablespoons olive oil
800g beef eye fillet
1 large kumara (500g)
2 large russet burbank potatoes (600g)
80g butter
2 tablespoons olive oil, extra
30g butter, extra
200g swiss brown mushrooms, halved
200g enoki mushrooms, trimmed
150g oyster mushrooms, halved
200g crème fraîche
3 green onions, sliced thinly
⅓ cup firmly packed fresh flat-leaf parsley leaves

1 Preheat oven to 200°C/180°C fan-forced.
2 Heat oil in large shallow flameproof baking dish; cook beef, uncovered, until browned all over. Roast, uncovered, in oven about 35 minutes or until cooked as desired. Cover to keep warm.
3 Meanwhile, coarsely grate kumara and potatoes into large bowl. Using hands, squeeze out excess moisture from potato mixture; shape mixture into eight portions. Heat 10g of the butter and 1 teaspoon of the extra oil in medium frying pan; spread one portion of the potato mixture over base of pan, flatten with spatula to form a firm pancake-like rösti. Cook, uncovered, over medium heat until browned; invert rösti onto large plate then gently slide back into pan to cook other side. Drain on absorbent paper; cover to keep warm. Repeat process with remaining butter, oil and potato mixture.
4 Heat extra butter in same cleaned pan; cook mushrooms, stirring, until just tender. Add crème fraîche; bring to the boil. Reduce heat; simmer, stirring, until sauce thickens slightly. Remove from heat; stir in onion and parsley.
5 Serve sliced beef with rösti and mushrooms.

preparation time 20 minutes **cooking time** 45 minutes **serves** 4
nutritional count per serving 69.9g total fat (34.1g saturated fat); 4080kJ (976 cal); 34.4g carbohydrate; 54.2g protein; 8.4g fibre

Sri lankan spicy beef ribs with coconut pilaf

1.6kg american-style spareribs (order in advance from the butcher)
¼ cup (60ml) peanut oil
¼ cup (60ml) white vinegar
1 teaspoon sambal oelek
1 teaspoon ground turmeric
4 cloves
½ teaspoon ground cardamom
3 cloves garlic, crushed
2 teaspoons grated fresh ginger
1 small brown onion (80g), chopped finely
coconut pilaf
40g butter
1 medium brown onion (150g), chopped coarsely
1 medium carrot (120g), chopped coarsely
2 cups (400g) basmati rice, washed, drained
1 litre (4 cups) chicken stock
¼ cup firmly packed fresh coriander leaves
¼ cup (10g) flaked coconut
¼ cup (40g) raisins

1 Using kitchen scissors, cut ribs into sections. Combine ribs in large bowl with combined remaining ingredients. Cover; refrigerate 3 hours or overnight.
2 Preheat oven to 240°C/220°C fan-forced.
3 Drain ribs; reserve marinade. Place ribs on oiled wire rack over large shallow baking dish. Roast, uncovered, brushing frequently with reserved marinade, about 30 minutes or until browned and cooked through, turning once halfway through cooking time.
4 Meanwhile, make coconut pilaf; serve ribs on pilaf.
coconut pilaf heat butter in medium saucepan; cook onion and carrot, stirring, until onion softens. Add rice; cook, stirring, 1 minute. Add stock; bring to the boil. Reduce heat; simmer, covered, about 20 minutes or until rice is just tender. Remove from heat; fluff rice with fork. Stir in coriander, coconut and raisins, cover; stand 5 minutes before serving.
preparation time 20 minutes (plus refrigeration time)
cooking time 35 minutes (plus standing time) **serves** 4
nutritional count per serving 35.9g total fat (14.5g saturated fat); 3775kJ (903 cal); 93.3g carbohydrate; 49.3g protein; 3.8g fibre

Mediterranean roast beef and vegetables

1.5kg piece fresh eye of silverside beef
⅓ cup (80ml) extra virgin olive oil
6 whole baby onions (150g)
3 medium zucchini (360g), halved lengthways
6 medium egg tomatoes (450g), halved
3 finger eggplants (180g), halved lengthways
2 medium yellow capsicums (400g), quartered
2 tablespoons balsamic vinegar
2 tablespoons shredded fresh basil
2 tablespoons chopped fresh tarragon
1 tablespoon drained baby capers

1 Preheat oven to 200°C/180°C fan-forced.
2 Rub beef with 2 teaspoons of the oil; sprinkle with salt and freshly ground black pepper. Heat 1 tablespoon of the oil in flameproof baking dish; cook beef until browned all over. Add onions to dish; roast, uncovered, in oven 20 minutes.
3 Place zucchini, tomato, eggplant and capsicum around beef in dish; roast further 40 minutes or until beef is cooked as desired. Remove beef from dish, cover with foil; stand 10 minutes.
4 Increase oven temperature to 240°C/220°C fan-forced; roast vegetables further 10 minutes or until browned and tender. Drizzle vegetables with combined remaining oil, vinegar, herbs and capers.
5 Serve thinly sliced beef with vegetable mixture.

preparation time 15 minutes
cooking time 1 hour 20 minutes (plus standing time) **serves** 6
nutritional count per serving 24.6g total fat (7.0g saturated fat); 2006kJ (480 cal); 5.6g carbohydrate; 57.5g protein; 3.3g fibre

Anchovy and garlic veal with roasted fennel

3 drained anchovy fillets
4 cloves garlic, chopped coarsely
3 teaspoons fresh rosemary leaves
1 teaspoon salt
1 teaspoon cracked black pepper
1 tablespoon olive oil
1kg rack of veal (8 cutlets)
2 medium red onions (340g), sliced thickly
2 bay leaves
8 baby fennel bulbs (1kg), trimmed, halved or quartered
½ cup (125ml) dry white wine
1 cup (250ml) chicken stock
12 small truss tomatoes (350g)

1 Preheat oven to 200°C/180°C fan-forced.
2 Using mortar and pestle or small blender, pound anchovies, garlic, rosemary, salt and pepper until mixture forms a paste; stir in oil. Rub anchovy mixture over veal. Cover; refrigerate for 1 hour.
3 Place onion and bay leaves in baking dish; place veal on top of onion. Place fennel around veal, add wine and stock; roast, uncovered, about 40 minutes or until veal is cooked as desired. Add extra stock if pan juices evaporate. Remove veal; cover to keep warm.
4 Meanwhile, add tomatoes to baking dish; roast, uncovered, with fennel further 15 minutes or until softened slightly. Discard bay leaves.
5 Serve veal with vegetables and pan juices.

preparation time 20 minutes (plus refrigeration time)
cooking time 55 minutes **serves** 4
nutritional count per serving 10.1g total fat (2.3g saturated fat); 1555kJ (372 cal); 11.6g carbohydrate; 50.1g protein; 6.7g fibre

Roast beef fillet with herb and walnut topping

750g piece beef fillet
1 tablespoon olive oil
½ cup coarsely chopped fresh flat-leaf parsley
¼ cup coarsely chopped fresh dill
1 clove garlic, crushed
2 teaspoons finely grated lemon rind
2 teaspoons lemon juice
¼ cup (30g) coarsely chopped roasted walnuts
1 tablespoon olive oil, extra

1 Preheat oven to 200°C/180°C fan-forced. Rub beef with oil.
2 Combine remaining ingredients in small bowl.
3 Cook beef, in flameproof baking dish, over high heat until browned all over. Roast, uncovered, in oven 15 minutes. Sprinkle beef with three-quarters of the herb and walnut mixture, cover; roast further 10 minutes or until cooked. Stand, covered, 10 minutes.
4 Serve sliced beef sprinkled with remaining herb and walnut mixture.

preparation time 20 minutes
cooking time 35 minutes (plus standing time) **serves** 6
nutritional count per serving 17.1g total fat (4.2g saturated fat); 1104kJ (264 cal); 0.3g carbohydrate; 27.2g protein; 0.7g fibre

Roasted beef eye fillet with red wine risotto

500g piece beef eye fillet
1 tablespoon olive oil
1 teaspoon ground black pepper
¼ cup (60ml) dry red wine
½ cup (125ml) beef stock
red wine risotto
3 cups (750ml) vegetable stock
40g butter
1 medium brown onion (150g), chopped finely
1 cup (200g) arborio rice
1 cup (250ml) dry red wine
¼ cup (20g) finely grated parmesan cheese
3 green onions, sliced thinly

1 Preheat oven to 200°C/180°C fan-forced
2 Trim excess fat from beef; tie beef with kitchen string at 3cm intervals. Place beef in oiled shallow flameproof baking dish; brush with oil, sprinkle with pepper. Roast, uncovered, 20 minutes or until cooked as desired.
3 Meanwhile, start making red wine risotto.
4 Remove beef from dish, cover; stand 10 minutes. Place baking dish over low heat, add wine; simmer, stirring, about 2 minutes or until mixture reduces by half. Add stock; stir until sauce comes to the boil. Strain sauce into small jug.
5 Serve sliced beef on risotto, drizzled with sauce.
red wine risotto place stock in medium saucepan; bring to the boil. Reduce heat; simmer, covered. Heat half of the butter in large saucepan; cook brown onion, stirring, until softened. Add rice; stir to coat rice in onion mixture. Add wine; bring to the boil. Reduce heat; simmer, stirring, 2 minutes. Stir in ½ cup of the simmering stock; cook, stirring, over low heat, until liquid is absorbed. Continue adding stock mixture, in ½-cup batches, stirring until absorbed after each addition. Total cooking time should be about 35 minutes or until rice is just tender. Add cheese, remaining butter and green onion, stirring until butter melts.

preparation time 15 minutes
cooking time 40 minutes (plus standing time) **serves** 4
nutritional count per serving 22.9g total fat (10.7g saturated fat); 2404kJ (575 cal); 43.5g carbohydrate; 35.1g protein; 1.1g fibre

Beef rib roast with potato puree and roasted beetroot

2kg beef standing rib roast
¼ cup (60ml) olive oil
sea salt flakes
2 teaspoons cracked pepper
600g small beetroot, scrubbed, trimmed
1kg sebago potatoes
40g butter, chopped
⅔ cup (160ml) milk, warmed
⅓ cup (80ml) cream, warmed
¼ cup finely grated fresh horseradish

1 Preheat oven to 220°C/200°C fan-forced.
2 Tie beef with kitchen string at 2cm intervals. Brush beef with 1 tablespoon of the oil; sprinkle with salt and pepper. Toss beetroot in remaining oil; add to dish. Roast, uncovered, about 20 minutes.
3 Reduce oven temperature to 180°C/160°C fan-forced; roast beef and beetroot, uncovered, further 1 hour or until beef is cooked as desired and beetroot are tender. Remove beef from dish; cover, stand 20 minutes. Continue roasting beetroot further 15 minutes or until tender.
4 Meanwhile, boil, steam or microwave potatoes until tender; drain. Mash potatoes; push through a sieve or mouli into a large bowl. Stir in butter then gradually beat in warmed milk and cream.
5 Serve beef with roasted beetroot, potato puree and horseradish.

preparation time 25 minutes
cooking time 1 hour 35 minutes (plus standing time) **serves** 4
nutritional count per serving 59.0g total fat (25.6g saturated fat); 4644kJ (1111 cal); 39.9g carbohydrate; 101.8g protein; 7.3g fibre

Veal rack with roast pumpkin risotto

1kg veal shin, cut into pieces
1 medium brown onion (150g), chopped coarsely
1 trimmed celery stalk (100g), chopped coarsely
1 medium carrot (120g), chopped coarsely
2 bay leaves
1 teaspoon black peppercorns
4 litres (16 cups) water
1.2kg veal rack (6 cutlet)
2 cloves garlic, crushed
2 tablespoons finely chopped fresh rosemary
2 tablespoons wholegrain mustard
1 tablespoon olive oil

1 Preheat oven to 220°C/200°C fan-forced. Place shin and onion in baking dish; roast, uncovered, 1 hour or until bones are well browned. Transfer bones and onion to large saucepan with celery, carrot, bay leaves, peppercorns and the water; bring to the boil. Reduce heat; simmer, uncovered, 3 hours. Strain stock through muslin-lined sieve into large bowl; discard solids. Cool, cover; refrigerate until cold.
2 Reduce oven temperature to 180°C/160°C fan-forced. Place veal rack on oiled wire rack over large shallow baking dish; spread with combined garlic, rosemary, mustard and oil. Roast, covered, 1 hour. Uncover; roast 30 minutes or until cooked as desired. Cover; stand 10 minutes.
3 Meanwhile, make roast pumpkin risotto; serve with cutlets.
roast pumpkin risotto place 500g coarsely chopped pumpkin on oven tray, drizzle with 1 tablespoon olive oil. Roast, uncovered, alongside veal for 45 minutes. Skim fat from stock, place in large saucepan, simmer, covered. Cook 1 finely chopped medium brown onion (150g) in 1 tablespoon olive oil in large saucepan, stir in 1½ cups (300g) arborio rice, then ½ cup (125ml) dry white wine, cook, stirring until liquid is absorbed. Stir in ½ cup of simmering stock, stir over low heat until absorbed. Continue adding stock in ½-cup batches, stirring, until absorbed between additions, this should take about 35 minutes. Stir in pumpkin, ¼ cup (20g) finely grated parmesan cheese, 20g butter and ⅓ cup finely chopped flat-leaf parsley.
preparation time 30 minutes (plus refrigeration time)
cooking time 5 hours 30 minutes **serves** 6
nutritional count per serving 17.8g total fat (5.3g saturated fat); 2700kJ (646 cal); 47.3g carbohydrate; 68.3g protein; 3.1g fibre

Honey mustard roast beef and vegetables

4 cloves garlic, peeled
1.8kg corner piece beef topside roast
12 small sprigs fresh thyme
6 medium carrots (720g), halved
12 baby onions (300g), peeled
1 tablespoon wholegrain mustard
¼ cup (90g) honey
1 tablespoon olive oil

1 Preheat oven to 180°C/160°C fan-forced.
2 Cut each garlic clove into three slices. Make 12 small slits on fat side of beef; insert garlic and thyme into slits. Cut a narrow strip from top of 35cm x 48cm oven bag to use as a tie.
3 Place beef, carrot and onion in bag with combined remaining ingredients; close end with tie. Gently turn bag to coat beef and vegetables with mustard mixture. Place bag in large flameproof baking dish, pierce three holes near tie end; bake about 1½ hours or until beef is cooked as desired.
4 Carefully remove beef and vegetables from bag; stand, covered, in warm place, 10 minutes before serving.
5 Pour juices from oven bag into same dish; simmer, uncovered, over heat until reduced to ½ cup (125ml).
6 Serve beef and vegetables drizzled with mustard mixture.

preparation time 15 minutes
cooking time 1 hour 40 minutes (plus standing time) **serves** 6
nutritional count per serving 12.9g total fat (4.3g saturated fat); 1923kJ (460 cal); 17.6g carbohydrate; 66.2g protein; 2.8g fibre

Herb and mustard-seasoned beef fillet

50g butter, softened
2 cloves garlic, crushed
2 teaspoons finely chopped fresh rosemary
1 tablespoon finely chopped fresh flat-leaf parsley
1 tablespoon finely chopped seeded black olives
1 tablespoon coarsely chopped roasted pine nuts
¼ cup (70g) wholegrain mustard
650g piece beef eye fillet, trimmed
1 tablespoon extra virgin olive oil
¼ cup (70g) horseradish cream

1 Combine butter, garlic, herbs, olives, nuts and 2 tablespoons of the mustard in small bowl. Transfer to small piping bag fitted with medium plain tube.
2 Preheat oven to 200°C/180°C fan-forced.
3 Tie beef firmly with kitchen string at 2cm intervals. Using knife-sharpening steel or thick butcher's skewer, pierce beef through centre, lengthways. Pipe butter mixture into cavity.
4 Heat oil in medium flameproof baking dish; cook beef over high heat about 5 minutes or until browned all over. Roast, uncovered, 20 minutes or until cooked as desired. Cover with foil; stand 5 minutes.
5 Serve beef sliced with combined horseradish and remaining mustard.

preparation time 20 minutes
cooking time 20 minutes (plus standing time) **serves** 6
nutritional count per serving 19.6g total fat (8.5g saturated fat); 1200kJ (287 cal); 3.0g carbohydrate; 24.4g protein; 1.0g fibre

Slow roasted beef and garlic with mustard cream

18 baby onions (720g)
2.5kg piece beef bolar blade or chuck
2 tablespoons olive oil
½ cup (125ml) red wine
2 sprigs fresh thyme
2 bulbs garlic, tops removed
1 cup (250ml) beef stock
mustard cream
½ cup (120g) sour cream
2 tablespoons wholegrain mustard

1 Preheat oven to 120°C/100°C fan-forced.
2 Place onions in heatproof bowl; cover with boiling water and stand for 5 minutes. Drain, peel away the skins.
3 Brush beef all over with oil; cook in heated large flameproof baking dish until browned all over. Add wine, simmer, uncovered, until reduced by half. Remove dish from heat; sprinkle beef with thyme.
4 Add garlic, peeled onions and stock to dish, cover tightly; roast 2½ hours. Uncover; baste meat with pan juices. Roast, uncovered, further 2 hours. Cover; stand 30 minutes before slicing.
5 Combine ingredients for mustard cream in small bowl.
6 Serve beef with onions, garlic, strained pan juices, mustard cream and steamed green beans, if desired.

preparation time 15 minutes
cooking time 4 hours 35 minutes (plus standing time) **serves** 6
nutritional count per serving 33.5g total fat (14.1g saturated fat); 2876kJ (688 cal); 4.5g carbohydrate; 87.1g protein; 3.1g fibre

Roast veal rack with herb stuffing

1 small brown onion (80g), chopped finely
1 clove garlic, crushed
½ trimmed celery stalk (50g), chopped finely
¾ cup (45g) stale breadcrumbs
1 tablespoon dijon mustard
1 teaspoon finely chopped fresh thyme
1 tablespoon finely chopped fresh flat-leaf parsley
1 teaspoon finely grated lemon rind
2 teaspoons sea salt flakes
2 teaspoons cracked black pepper
800g veal rack (4 cutlets), trimmed
1 medium brown onion (150g), chopped coarsely
1½ cups (375ml) beef stock
2 teaspoons olive oil
2 teaspoons balsamic vinegar
½ cup (125ml) beef stock, extra

1 Preheat oven to 220°C/200°C fan-forced.
2 Cook finely chopped onion, garlic and celery in heated oiled small frying pan, stirring, until vegetables soften. Add breadcrumbs; cook until breadcrumbs brown lightly. Remove from heat; stir in mustard, herbs, rind, half of the salt and half of the pepper. Cool 10 minutes.
3 Using sharp knife, make a tunnel through veal rack, close to the bone; fill with herb mixture.
4 Place coarsely chopped onion and stock in large flameproof baking dish; add veal, drizzle with oil, sprinkle with remaining salt and pepper. Roast, uncovered, in oven about 30 minutes or until cooked as desired. Remove veal from dish, cover; stand 10 minutes.
5 Stir vinegar and extra stock into pan juices in dish; bring to the boil. Strain into medium jug; serve with veal and green beans, if desired.

preparation time 20 minutes
cooking time 35 minutes (plus cooling and standing time) **serves** 4
nutritional count per serving 6.8g total fat (1.7g saturated fat); 1145kJ (274 cal); 11.7g carbohydrate; 40.2g protein; 1.7g fibre

Slow-roasted veal breast with soft polenta

2 tablespoons olive oil
20g butter
2kg veal breast
2 medium brown onions (300g), chopped coarsely
2 cloves garlic, quartered
2 medium carrots (240g), chopped coarsely
4 trimmed celery stalks (400g), chopped coarsely
6 sprigs fresh rosemary
1 cup (250ml) dry white wine
1 cup (250ml) beef stock
soft polenta
1.5 litres (6 cups) water
2 teaspoons salt
2 cups (340g) polenta
½ cup (125ml) milk
½ cup (40g) grated parmesan cheese

1 Heat oil and butter in large flameproof baking dish; cook veal until browned all over, remove from dish.
2 Preheat oven to 160°C/140°C fan-forced.
3 Cook onion and garlic in same dish, stirring, until soft. Stir in carrot, celery and rosemary; cook, stirring, until softened slightly. Add combined wine and stock; bring to the boil. Return veal to dish, cover tightly; roast in oven about 3 hours or until tender.
4 Make soft polenta.
5 Serve veal slices with soft polenta; top with vegetables and drizzle with pan juices.
soft polenta bring the water and salt to the boil in large saucepan. Gradually stir in polenta then simmer, uncovered, about 25 minutes or until thick, stirring constantly. Add milk; cook, stirring, about 5 minutes or until mixture is thick. Stir in cheese.

preparation time 20 minutes **cooking time** 3 hours 20 minutes
serves 8
nutritional count per serving 13.6g total fat (4.6g saturated fat); 2266kJ (542 cal); 34.3g carbohydrate; 63.1g protein; 3.3g fibre

Pepper-crusted beef fillet with vegetable and polenta chips

3 cups (750ml) water
¾ cup (120g) polenta
¼ cup (70g) wholegrain mustard
2 teaspoons cracked black pepper
600g beef eye fillet
1 large kumara (500g), peeled, cut into batons
2 large parsnips (700g), peeled, cut into batons
2 large carrots (360g), peeled, cut into batons
2 teaspoons olive oil
cooking-oil spray
½ cup coarsely chopped fresh flat-leaf parsley
¼ cup (60ml) balsamic vinegar
¼ cup (60ml) water, extra
1 tablespoon honey

1 Oil deep 23cm-square cake pan. Bring the water to the boil in saucepan. Gradually add polenta to liquid, stirring constantly. Reduce heat; cook, stirring constantly, 10 minutes or until polenta thickens. Stir in 1 tablespoon of the mustard; spread polenta into pan. Cover; refrigerate 1 hour or until firm.
2 Preheat oven to 200°C/180°C fan-forced.
3 Combine pepper and 1 tablespoon of the mustard; spread all over beef. Combine vegetables, in single layer, in large shallow flameproof baking dish; drizzle with oil. Roast, uncovered, 10 minutes. Add beef; roast, uncovered, 35 minutes or until vegetables are crisp and beef is cooked as desired.
4 Meanwhile, turn polenta onto board; cut into batons similar to vegetables. Place, in single layer, on oven tray; coat with cooking oil spray. Bake alongside beef for last 20 minutes of cooking time or until browned lightly.
5 Remove beef from baking dish. Cover beef; stand 5 minutes before slicing thinly. Place vegetables in large bowl with parsley; toss gently to combine. Cover to keep warm.
6 Cook vinegar, the extra water, honey and remaining mustard in same dish over high heat, stirring, 5 minutes or until sauce bubbles and thickens.
7 Serve beef on polenta and vegetables, drizzled with sauce.
preparation time 20 minutes (plus refrigeration time)
cooking time 1 hour 5 minutes   **serves** 4
nutritional count per serving 11.1g total fat (3.3g saturated fat); 2140kJ (512 cal); 61.1g carbohydrate; 40.7g protein; 9.6g fibre

Slow-roasted beef shanks

1 large beef shank (2.5kg), quartered crossways
2 tablespoons plain flour
2 tablespoons olive oil
2 x 425g cans crushed tomatoes
½ cup (125ml) dry white wine
½ cup (125ml) beef stock
¼ cup (70g) tomato paste
¼ cup finely chopped fresh flat-leaf parsley
2 tablespoons finely chopped fresh lemon thyme

1 Preheat oven to 180°C/160°C fan-forced.
2 Toss shank pieces in flour; shake away excess. Heat oil in large frying pan; cook shank pieces, in batches, until browned and almost crunchy all over.
3 Place undrained tomatoes, wine, stock and paste in deep 5-litre (20 cup) baking dish; stir to combine. Place shank pieces, one at a time, standing upright, in dish; roast, covered, about 2 hours or until tender.
4 Remove shanks from dish. When cool enough to handle, remove meat from bones. Discard bones; chop meat coarsely. Return meat to dish with tomato sauce; reheat if necessary. Stir in herbs just before serving.
5 Serve shanks with risotto, if desired.

preparation time 30 minutes **cooking time** 2 hours 45 minutes
serves 6
nutritional count per serving 18.8g total fat (6.1g saturated fat); 1701kJ (407 cal); 8.5g carbohydrate; 46.4g protein; 2.4g fibre
tip ask your butcher to quarter the beef shank crossways so that the pieces will fit into the baking dish.

Veal rack with rosemary and rocket pesto

1kg baby new potatoes
1 clove garlic, quartered
50g baby rocket leaves
¼ cup (60ml) extra virgin olive oil
¼ cup coarsely chopped fresh rosemary
1kg veal rack (8 cutlets)
½ cup (40g) finely grated parmesan cheese
1 tablespoon plain flour
¾ cup (180ml) beef stock
¼ cup (60ml) dry white wine
1 tablespoon redcurrant jelly
500g asparagus, trimmed

1 Preheat oven to 200°C/180°C fan-forced.
2 Place potatoes in oiled shallow medium baking dish; roast, uncovered, about 50 minutes or until tender.
3 Meanwhile, blend or process garlic, rocket, oil and 2 tablespoons of the rosemary until mixture forms a paste. Stir remaining rosemary into pesto. Place veal on oiled wire rack over large shallow flameproof baking dish; spread pesto all over veal. Roast, uncovered, about 40 minutes or until veal is browned and cooked as desired. Remove veal from dish; cover to keep warm.
4 When potatoes are tender, sprinkle with cheese; roast, uncovered, about 5 minutes or until cheese melts.
5 Place flameproof dish with pan juices over heat, add flour; cook, stirring, until mixture thickens and bubbles. Gradually add stock, wine and jelly, stirring, until sauce boils and thickens slightly.
6 Meanwhile, boil, steam or microwave asparagus until just tender; drain.
7 Serve veal, sliced into cutlets, with potatoes, asparagus and sauce.

preparation time 15 minutes
cooking time 1 hour 5 minutes (plus standing time) **serves** 4
nutritional count per serving 22.1g total fat (5.4g saturated fat); 2596kJ (621 cal); 41.2g carbohydrate; 58.2g protein; 6.8g fibre

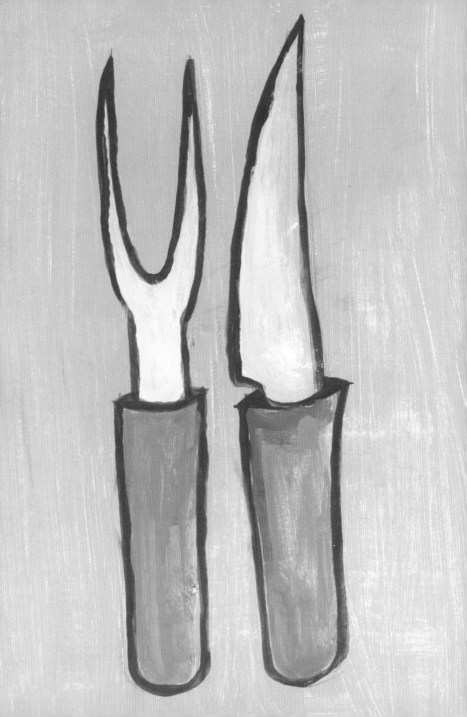

lamb

Spring roast lamb with mint sauce

2 tablespoons extra virgin olive oil
4 cloves garlic, crushed
2 tablespoons lemon juice
2 tablespoons fresh oregano leaves
2kg tunnel-boned leg lamb
1kg desiree potatoes, cut into wedges
1 cup (250ml) chicken stock
2 sprigs fresh rosemary stems
mint sauce
2 cups firmly packed fresh mint leaves
2 tablespoons almond meal
2 cloves garlic, quartered
⅓ cup (80ml) extra virgin olive oil
2 tablespoons lemon juice

1 Combine oil, garlic, juice and oregano in small bowl. Rub lamb all over with garlic mixture, inside and out. Cover; refrigerate 3 hours or overnight.
2 Preheat oven to 200°C/180°C fan-forced.
3 Place potatoes in large oiled baking dish. Pour stock over potatoes; top with rosemary sprigs. Place lamb on top of potatoes. Roast, uncovered, about 1 hour or until lamb is cooked as desired. Remove lamb from dish; cover, stand 15 minutes.
4 Increase oven temperature to 240°C/230°C fan-forced; roast potatoes further 15 minutes or until browned.
5 Make mint sauce.
6 Serve lamb with potatoes and sauce, and red coleslaw, if desired.
mint sauce blend or process mint, almond meal and garlic until finely chopped. Transfer mixture to small bowl; stir in oil and juice.

preparation time 20 minutes (plus refrigeration time)
cooking time 1 hour 15 minutes **serves** 6
nutritional count per serving 38.4g total fat (10.8g saturated fat);
3114kJ (745 cal); 19.3g carbohydrate; 78.7g protein; 4.1g fibre

Spice-crusted lamb racks with potato wedges

5 medium potatoes (1kg), cut into wedges
¼ cup (60ml) olive oil
4 x 4 french-trimmed cutlet lamb racks (600g)
½ teaspoon dried chilli flakes
2 tablespoons kalonji seeds
2 tablespoons sesame seeds
1 clove garlic, crushed
½ cup loosely packed fresh flat-leaf parsley leaves

1 Preheat oven to 200°C/180°C fan-forced.
2 Combine potato and 2 tablespoons of the oil on oven tray. Roast potato, in single layer, uncovered, about 55 minutes or until browned lightly and crisp.
3 Meanwhile, place lamb on separate oven tray; rub all over with combined remaining oil, chilli, seeds and garlic. Roast, uncovered, for last 20 minutes of potato cooking time or until lamb is browned and cooked as desired.
4 Combine potatoes and parsley in large bowl; serve with lamb and lemon, if desired.

preparation time 15 minutes **cooking time** 55 minutes **serves** 4
nutritional count per serving 31.6g total fat (8.4g saturated fat); 2044kJ (489 cal); 28.9g carbohydrate; 22.4g protein; 4.8g fibre

Spiced roast lamb with coconut rice

¼ teaspoon ground turmeric
2 teaspoons cumin seeds, crushed
1 teaspoon ground coriander
2 teaspoons finely grated lemon rind
2 tablespoons lemon juice
2 cloves garlic, crushed
1 tablespoon honey, warmed
1 teaspoon salt
1.5kg easy carve leg of lamb
2 cups (500ml) water
coconut rice
1½ cups (300g) basmati rice
400ml coconut milk
1½ cups (375ml) chicken stock
4 fresh dates, sliced thinly
¼ cup (35g) slivered almonds, roasted
80g baby spinach leaves

1 Dry-fry turmeric, cumin and coriander in small frying pan, stirring, about 1 minute or until fragrant. Combine spices, rind, juice, garlic, honey and salt in small bowl. Place lamb in shallow baking tray; rub or brush spice mixture all over lamb. Cover; refrigerate several hours or overnight.
2 Preheat oven to 180°C/160°C fan-forced.
3 Place lamb on oiled wire rack in medium baking dish; pour the water into dish. Roast, uncovered, about 1 hour 10 minutes or until lamb is cooked as desired. Cover; stand 15 minutes. Skim fat from pan juices.
4 Meanwhile, make coconut rice.
5 Serve lamb and juices with rice.
coconut rice place rice in large bowl, fill with cold water and stir with hand. Drain, repeat process two to three times or until water runs clear. Drain rice in sieve. Place drained rice, coconut milk and stock in medium saucepan; cover, bring to the boil. Reduce heat; simmer, covered tightly, over low heat 12 minutes or until liquid is absorbed. Remove from heat. Stir in dates, almonds and spinach.

preparation time 20 minutes (plus refrigeration time)
cooking time 1 hour 10 minutes **serves** 6
nutritional count per serving 27.6g total fat (16.9g saturated fat); 2721kJ (651 cal); 50.9g carbohydrate; 47.9g protein; 3.2g fibre

Harissa lamb leg and warm couscous salad

30g dried red chillies, chopped coarsely
1 teaspoon ground cumin
1 teaspoon ground coriander
1 teaspoon caraway seeds
2 cloves garlic, crushed
⅓ cup (90g) tomato puree
⅓ cup (80ml) olive oil
2kg leg of lamb
couscous salad
2 small kumara (500g), cut into 1cm pieces
cooking-oil spray
2 cups (400g) couscous
½ cup (60g) frozen peas, thawed
1 tablespoon finely grated lemon rind
2½ cups (625ml) boiling water
1 small red onion (100g), chopped finely
½ cup finely shredded fresh flat-leaf parsley
¼ cup finely shredded fresh mint
2 tablespoons olive oil
1 tablespoon red wine vinegar
¼ cup (60ml) lemon juice

1 Soak chilli in boiling water for 1 hour. Drain; reserve ¼ cup of the liquid.
2 Dry-fry spices in small frying pan. Blend spices with chilli, reserved liquid, garlic and puree. With motor operating, add oil in thin stream; blend until smooth. Reserve ⅓ cup harissa for another use.
3 Pierce lamb all over; rub with remaining harissa. Refrigerate 3 hours.
4 Preheat oven to 200°C/180°C fan-forced.
5 Pour enough water into large baking dish to 5mm depth. Place lamb on rack over dish; roast, uncovered, about 1 hour. Cover lamb; stand 20 minutes.
6 Meanwhile, make couscous salad; serve with sliced lamb.
couscous salad place kumara on oven tray; spray with cooking-oil. Roast alongside lamb for last 30 minutes. Combine couscous, peas, rind and the water in large heatproof bowl; cover, stand 5 minutes. Stir in kumara and remaining ingredients.
preparation time 40 minutes (plus standing and refrigeration time)
cooking time 1 hour 5 minutes **serves** 4
nutritional count per serving 49.0g total fat (12.9g saturated fat); 5150kJ (1232 cal); 98.1g carbohydrate; 98.7g protein; 5.6g fibre

Rolled lamb loin with tomato concasse

1 medium red capsicum (200g)
700g boned loin of lamb
2 cloves garlic, crushed
20g baby spinach leaves
⅓ cup loosely packed fresh basil leaves
1 tablespoon olive oil
tomato concasse
1 tablespoon olive oil
3 shallots (75g), chopped finely
4 cloves garlic, crushed
1.2kg large egg tomatoes, peeled, seeded, chopped finely
2 tablespoons red wine vinegar

1 Preheat oven to 240°C/220°C fan-forced.
2 Make tomato concasse.
3 Meanwhile, quarter capsicum; discard seeds and membranes. Roast in oven, skin-side up, until skin blisters and blackens. Cover capsicum in plastic wrap or paper for 5 minutes; peel away skin, slice capsicum thinly.
4 Reduce oven temperature to 180°C/160°C fan-forced.
5 Place lamb, cut-side up, on board; rub garlic into lamb then place capsicum, spinach and basil down centre of lamb; roll tightly, secure at 2cm intervals with kitchen string. Rub oil over lamb roll.
6 Place lamb on oiled wire rack over large shallow baking dish; roast, uncovered, about 1 hour or until lamb is browned and cooked as desired. Cover to keep warm.
7 Serve thickly sliced lamb with concasse and, if desired, peas.
tomato concasse heat oil in medium saucepan; cook shallot and garlic, stirring, until shallot softens. Add tomato and vinegar; cook, covered, over low heat, 15 minutes. Uncover; simmer, stirring occasionally, 30 minutes or until mixture thickens slightly.

preparation time 30 minutes
cooking time 1 hour 30 minutes (plus standing time) **serves** 4
nutritional count per serving 20.3g total fat (7.7g saturated fat); 1526kJ (365 cal); 5.0g carbohydrate; 39.1g protein; 3.1g fibre

Roasted spiced lamb and vegetables

2 x 350g mini lamb roasts
1 tablespoon olive oil
250g cherry tomatoes
2 medium zucchini (240g), halved lengthways
250g baby red capsicums or 1 large red capsicum (350g), quartered
spice rub
2 tablespoons olive oil
1 teaspoon dried oregano leaves
3 cloves garlic, crushed
¼ teaspoon salt
1 teaspoon sweet paprika
1 tablespoon lemon juice

1 Preheat oven to very hot (240°C/220°C fan-forced).
2 Combine ingredients for spice rub in small bowl; rub half of the spice rub over lamb.
3 Heat oil in medium flameproof baking dish; cook lamb, over heat, until browned all over. Roast, uncovered, in oven for 10 minutes.
4 Combine remaining spice rub with vegetables in medium baking dish; roast alongside lamb 15 minutes. Remove lamb; cover, stand 10 minutes.
5 Roast vegetables further 5 minutes or until tender.
6 Serve lamb with vegetables.

preparation time 15 minutes **cooking time** 35 minutes **serves** 4
nutritional count per serving 29.5g total fat (8.9g saturated fat);
1852kJ (443 cal); 4.9g carbohydrate; 38.7g protein; 3.1g fibre

Garlic and sage lamb racks

3 large red onions (900g)
12 fresh sage leaves
⅓ cup (80ml) olive oil
2 tablespoons coarsely chopped fresh sage
4 cloves garlic, chopped coarsely
4 x 4 french-trimmed cutlet lamb racks (600g)

1 Preheat oven to 220°C/200°C fan-forced.
2 Halve onions, slice into thin wedges; place in large baking dish with sage leaves and half of the oil.
3 Combine remaining oil in small bowl with chopped sage and garlic. Press sage mixture all over lamb; place on onion in dish.
4 Roast, uncovered, about 25 minutes or until lamb is browned all over and cooked as desired. Cover lamb racks; stand 10 minutes.

preparation time 10 minutes
cooking time 25 minutes (plus standing time) **serves** 4
nutritional count per serving 31.3g fat (8.5g saturated fat); 1676kJ (401 cal); 12.4g carbohydrate; 18.4g protein; 3.4g fibre
tip red onions are sweet and have a less aggressive flavour than their brown and white counterparts.

Slow-cooked lamb shoulder

2 tablespoons olive oil
1.2kg lamb shoulder
2 medium brown onions (300g), chopped coarsely
2 medium carrots (240g), chopped coarsely
2 trimmed celery stalks (200g), chopped coarsely
1 tablespoon white sugar
½ cup (125ml) dry red wine
½ cup (125ml) lamb stock
10 sprigs fresh oregano

1 Preheat oven to 150°C/130°C fan-forced.
2 Heat oil in large flameproof baking dish; cook lamb, uncovered, over high heat until browned all over. Remove lamb from dish.
3 Cook onion, carrot and celery in same dish, stirring, until browned lightly. Add sugar; cook, stirring, 1 minute. Add wine and stock; bring to the boil, then remove from heat.
4 Place half of the oregano on vegetables; place lamb on top, then place remaining oregano on lamb. Roast, covered tightly, 1½ hours. Turn lamb; roast, covered, another 1½ hours. Turn again; roast, covered, further 1 hour. Remove lamb from dish; cover with foil to keep warm.
5 Strain dish contents, discarding vegetables, oregano and as much fat as possible. Serve lamb with strained hot pan juices.

preparation time 15 minutes   **cooking time** 4 hours 15 minutes
serves 4
nutritional count per serving 29.1g total fat (10.4g saturated fat); 2149kJ (514 cal); 11.7g carbohydrate; 45.0g protein; 3.2g fibre
tip beef stock can be substituted for lamb stock, and rosemary can be substituted for oregano.

Lamb shanks in five-spice, tamarind and ginger

2 teaspoons five-spice powder
1 teaspoon dried chilli flakes
1 cinnamon stick
2 star anise
¼ cup (60ml) soy sauce
½ cup (125ml) chinese cooking wine
2 tablespoons tamarind concentrate
2 tablespoons brown sugar
8cm piece fresh ginger (40g), grated
2 cloves garlic, chopped coarsely
1¼ cups (310ml) water
8 french-trimmed lamb shanks (1.6kg)
500g choy sum, cut into 10cm lengths
150g sugar snap peas, trimmed

1 Preheat oven to 180ºC/160ºC fan-forced.
2 Dry-fry five-spice, chilli, cinnamon and star anise in small frying pan, stirring, until fragrant. Combine spices with soy sauce, wine, tamarind, sugar, ginger, garlic and the water in medium jug.
3 Place shanks, in single layer, in large shallow baking dish; drizzle with spice mixture. Roast, uncovered, turning shanks occasionally, about 2 hours or until meat is almost falling off the bone. Remove shanks from dish; cover to keep warm. Skim away excess fat from pan juices; strain sauce into small saucepan.
4 Meanwhile, boil, steam or microwave choy sum and peas, separately, until tender; drain.
5 Divide vegetables among serving plates; serve with shanks, drizzled with reheated sauce.

preparation time 20 minutes **cooking time** 2 hours 10 minutes
serves 4
nutritional count per serving 20.0g total fat (9.0g saturated fat); 1885kJ (451 cal); 12.5g carbohydrate; 48.3g protein; 3.1g fibre

Duxelles-filled lamb leg with roast vegetables

A duxelles (doo-zell) is a classic French mixture of finely chopped shallots and mushrooms cooked in butter, often used in pâtés and stuffings.

40g butter
1 clove garlic, crushed
3 shallots (75g), chopped finely
150g swiss brown mushrooms, chopped finely
½ cup (125ml) balsamic vinegar
1.2kg easy carve leg of lamb
1 teaspoon sea salt
2 large parsnips (700g)
2 large carrots (360g)
1 large kumara (500g)
2 large potatoes (600g)
2 tablespoons olive oil
½ cup (125ml) beef stock

1 Melt butter in large frying pan; cook garlic, shallots and mushrooms, stirring, until shallot softens. Add half of the vinegar; bring to the boil. Reduce heat; simmer duxelles, uncovered, about 5 minutes or until liquid has evaporated. Fill lamb cavity with duxelles; rub lamb all over with salt.
2 Preheat oven to 180°C/160°C fan-forced.
3 Halve parsnips, carrots and kumara first crossways, then lengthways; cut pieces into thick slices. Cut potatoes into wedges. Place vegetables, in single layer, in large shallow flameproof baking dish; drizzle with oil.
4 Place lamb on oiled wire rack over vegetables; roast, uncovered, about 1½ hours or until lamb is cooked as desired and vegetables are tender. Remove lamb and vegetables from dish, cover lamb; stand 10 minutes.
5 Meanwhile, place dish containing juices over heat; stir in stock and remaining vinegar, bring to the boil. Strain sauce into small jug.
6 Serve lamb with vegetables, drizzled with sauce.

preparation time 30 minutes **cooking time** 1 hour 45 minutes
serves 4
nutritional count per serving 34.3g total fat (13.9g saturated fat); 3432kJ (821 cal); 50.5g carbohydrate; 76.5g protein; 11.0g fibre

Lamb wrapped in banana leaf

1 cup coarsely chopped fresh coriander leaves
2 coriander roots, chopped finely
10cm stick fresh lemon grass (20g), chopped finely
2 cloves garlic, crushed
1 teaspoon finely grated lime rind
2 tablespoons lime juice
1 fresh small red thai chilli, chopped finely
1 tablespoon grated palm sugar
2 tablespoons fish sauce
2 mini lamb roasts (700g)
2 large banana leaves
cooking-oil spray

1 Combine chopped fresh coriander, coriander root, lemon grass, garlic, rind, juice, chilli, sugar and sauce in large bowl; add lamb, turn to coat in marinade. Cover; refrigerate 3 hours or overnight.
2 Preheat oven to 180°C/160°C fan-forced.
3 Strain marinade from lamb through fine sieve over medium bowl; reserve marinade solids in strainer, discard marinade. Cut each lamb roast in half horizontally.
4 Trim banana leaves into four 30cm squares. Using tongs, dip one square at a time into large saucepan of boiling water, remove immediately. Rinse under cold water; pat dry with absorbent paper. Banana leaf squares should be soft and pliable.
5 Using fingers, press lamb halves all over with marinade solids; place each half in the centre of one of the banana leaf squares. Fold leaf over lamb to enclose; secure each parcel with kitchen string.
6 Place lamb parcels, in single layer, in large shallow baking dish; spray parcels with cooking-oil spray. Bake, uncovered, about 30 minutes or until lamb is cooked as desired.
7 Serve lamb on opened banana leaf with a thai-style salad, if desired.

preparation time 50 minutes (plus refrigeration time)
cooking time 25 minutes **serves** 4
nutritional count per serving 16.3g total fat (7.1g saturated fat); 1325kJ (317 cal); 4.3g carbohydrate; 37.9g protein; 0.8g fibre
tip banana leaves can be ordered from greengrocers.

Lamb cutlets in harissa with couscous

8 fresh small red thai chillies, chopped coarsely
4 cloves garlic, quartered
1 teaspoon salt
2 tablespoons coriander seeds
1 tablespoon cumin seeds
2 teaspoons caraway seeds
1 tablespoon coarsely grated lemon rind
1 tablespoon lemon juice
¼ cup (60ml) olive oil
2 x 6 cutlet lamb racks (450g)
⅓ cup (80ml) olive oil, extra
8 saffron threads
2 cups (400g) couscous
20g butter, chopped
2 cups (500ml) boiling water
2 tablespoons finely chopped rinsed preserved lemon
100g cracked green olives, chopped coarsely
¼ cup fresh mint leaves, shredded finely
½ cup (70g) slivered almonds, roasted
200g sheep-milk yogurt

1 Preheat oven to 240°C/220°C fan-forced.
2 Blend or process chilli, garlic, salt, seeds, rind, juice and oil until mixture forms a paste.
3 Cut slits between cutlets with sharp knife; push 1 teaspoon of the harissa paste in each slit, press remaining harissa over outside of racks. Place racks in large oiled baking dish; roast, uncovered, 35 minutes or until browned and cooked as desired. Cover racks; stand 5 minutes before slicing into cutlets.
4 Meanwhile, heat extra oil in small saucepan; stir in saffron. Remove from heat, cool; strain through fine strainer into small jug.
5 Combine couscous, butter and the water in large heatproof bowl; fluff with fork to separate grains. Stir in lemon, olives, mint and almonds.
6 Serve cutlets with couscous and yogurt; drizzle with saffron oil.

preparation time 20 minutes **cooking time** 35 minutes **serves** 4
nutritional count per serving 54.7g total fat (11.8g saturated fat); 4042kJ (967 cal); 86.5g carbohydrate; 30.6g protein; 4.1g fibre

Tunnel-boned lamb with coriander hazelnut pesto

Ask the butcher to bone the lamb shoulder for you.

⅓ cup (50g) unroasted hazelnuts
½ cup firmly packed fresh coriander leaves
⅓ cup firmly packed fresh basil leaves
4cm piece fresh ginger (20cm), grated
5 cloves garlic, crushed
2 tablespoons lime juice
2 teaspoons fish sauce
1 teaspoon brown sugar
2 tablespoons olive oil
1.7kg lamb shoulder, boned

1 Preheat oven to 200°C/180°C fan-forced.
2 Spread nuts in single layer on oven tray; roast, uncovered, 5 minutes or until skins begin to flake. Rub nuts in soft cloth to remove skins; cool.
3 Reduce oven temperature to 180°C/160°C fan-forced.
4 Blend or process roasted nuts, herbs, ginger, garlic, juice, sauce and sugar until smooth. With motor operating, add oil in thin, steady stream; process until pesto thickens.
5 Spread lamb with half of the pesto. Roll from short side to enclose pesto; secure lamb with skewers, tie with kitchen string at 2cm intervals. Place lamb on oiled wire rack in large baking dish; spread remaining pesto all over lamb. Roast, uncovered, about 1¾ hours or until cooked as desired. Cover; stand 10 minutes. Remove and discard skewers.

preparation time 30 minutes
cooking time 1 hour 50 minutes (plus cooling time) **serves** 6
nutritional count per serving 30.0g total fat (9.7g saturated fat); 1864kJ (446 cal); 1.6g carbohydrate; 42.2g protein; 1.5g fibre

Roast lamb with tomato and potatoes

2.5kg leg of lamb, shank intact
6 cloves garlic, sliced
6 sprigs thyme, cut into 2cm pieces
2 tablespoons olive oil
4 medium brown onions (540g), chopped coarsely
6 medium tomatoes (900g), peeled, seeded, chopped
2 bay leaves
⅓ cup (80ml) brandy
2 cups (500ml) dry white wine
8 medium washed potatoes (1.2kg), quartered
1 cup (250ml) chicken stock

1 Pierce lamb 12 times with a sharp knife; press a slice of garlic and a piece of thyme into each cut. Reserve remaining garlic and thyme.
2 Preheat oven to 180°C/160°C fan-forced.
3 Heat half of the oil in a large flameproof baking dish; cook lamb until browned all over. Remove lamb from dish.
4 Heat remaining oil in same dish; cook onion, reserved garlic and thyme until soft but not coloured. Add tomatoes; cook, stirring, until softened. Add bay leaves, brandy and wine; bring to the boil.
5 Return lamb to dish; roast, uncovered, in oven 30 minutes. Add potatoes to same dish; roast, uncovered, further 1 hour 10 minutes or until lamb is cooked as desired and potatoes are tender. Spoon pan juices over the lamb occasionally during cooking. Remove lamb from dish. Cover with foil; stand 15 minutes.
6 Meanwhile, strain pan juices into medium saucepan; reserve tomato mixture and cover to keep warm. Skim fat from top of juices in saucepan. Add stock; bring to the boil. Boil, uncovered, 5 minutes or until reduced to 1½ cups (375ml).
7 Serve lamb with potatoes, reserved tomato mixture and sauce.

preparation time 20 minutes **cooking time** 1 hour 40 minutes
serves 8
nutritional count per serving 17.5g total fat (6.3g saturated fat); 2232kJ (534 cal); 20.9g carbohydrate; 56.0g protein; 3.7g fibre

Honey dijon lamb racks with potato and kumara gratin

2 tablespoons olive oil
2 teaspoons dijon mustard
¼ cup (60ml) red wine vinegar
2 cloves garlic, crushed
2 tablespoons honey
4 x 4 french-trimmed lamb cutlet racks (600g)
1 medium kumara (400g)
2 medium potatoes (400g)
1 tablespoon plain flour
1¾ cups (430ml) cream
¼ cup (60ml) milk
¾ cup (75g) grated pizza cheese

1 Combine oil, mustard, vinegar, garlic and honey in large bowl; add lamb, turn to coat all over in marinade. Cover; refrigerate 3 hours or overnight.
2 Preheat oven to 200°C/180°C fan-forced. Oil deep 19cm-square cake pan.
3 Using V-slicer, mandoline or sharp knife, cut kumara and potatoes into 2mm-thick slices; place half of the kumara slices, overlapping slightly, in pan. Top with a layer using half of the potato, overlapping slices slightly. Repeat layering with remaining kumara and potato.
4 Blend flour with a little of the cream in medium jug to form a smooth paste; stir in remaining cream and milk. Pour cream mixture over potato and kumara. Cover gratin with foil; bake about 45 minutes or until vegetables are tender. Uncover; sprinkle with cheese. Bake, uncovered, 15 minutes or until cheese browns lightly. Stand 5 minutes before serving.
5 Meanwhile, drain lamb; reserve marinade. Place lamb on oiled wire rack in large shallow baking dish; roast, uncovered, for about the last 35 minutes of gratin cooking time or until cooked as desired. Cover to keep warm.
6 Bring reserved marinade to the boil in small saucepan. Reduce heat; simmer sauce, uncovered, 5 minutes.
7 Serve gratin with lamb, drizzled with sauce.

preparation time 40 minutes (plus refrigeration time)
cooking time 1 hour 10 minutes **serves** 4
nutritional count per serving 66.5g total fat (36.2g saturated fat); 3632kJ (869 cal); 42.0g carbohydrate; 27.6g protein; 3.4g fibre

Slow-roasted lamb shoulder

1.5kg lamb shoulder, with shank intact
1½ tablespoons olive oil
30g butter
1kg potatoes, sliced thinly
2 medium brown onions (300g), sliced thinly
4 drained anchovy fillets, chopped finely
2 bulbs garlic
2 tablespoons fresh rosemary leaves
2 tablespoons white wine vinegar
2 cups (500ml) water

1 Preheat oven to 180°C/160°C fan-forced.
2 Trim excess fat from lamb. Heat a heavy flameproof baking dish over a moderately high heat. Add oil and butter, then lamb; cook until lamb is well browned all over. Remove lamb from dish.
3 Layer potato, onion and anchovies in same dish. Remove papery skin from garlic, cut bulbs is half crossways; place on potatoes.
4 Place lamb on top of potatoes; sprinkle with rosemary and vinegar, add the water. Cover dish tightly with two layers of foil; roast 1½ hours. Remove foil, reduce oven temperature to 160°C/140°C fan-forced; roast further 1½ hours. Remove lamb, cover; stand 10 minutes.
5 Serve lamb with potatoes and half a bulb of garlic.

preparation time 20 minutes (plus standing time)
cooking time 3 hours 30 minutes **serves** 4
nutritional count per serving 39.5g total fat (16.8g saturated fat); 3210kJ (768 cal); 34.8g carbohydrate; 63.1g protein; 11.3g fibre
tip if desired, while the lamb is resting, increase the oven temperature to 220°C/200°C fan-forced and roast potatoes for a further 10 minutes or until browned.

Jerk mini lamb roasts with black bean salad

2 mini lamb roasts (700g)
1 cup (200g) dried black beans
¼ cup (60ml) olive oil
1 large brown onion (200g), chopped finely
1 clove garlic, crushed
1 fresh long green chilli, chopped finely
1 teaspoon ground cumin
2 tablespoons red wine vinegar
1 large tomato (220g), seeded, chopped coarsely
½ cup firmly packed fresh coriander leaves
3 green onions, sliced thinly
2 tablespoons lime juice
jerk marinade
3 fresh long green chillies, chopped finely
3 green onions, chopped finely
2 cloves garlic, crushed
1 tablespoon soy sauce
1 tablespoon lime juice
1 teaspoon ground allspice
1 teaspoon dried thyme
1 teaspoon white sugar

1 Combine ingredients for jerk marinade in large bowl; rub all over lamb. Cover; refrigerate overnight. Soak beans in medium bowl of water overnight.
2 Preheat oven to 180ºC/160ºC fan-forced.
3 Drain beans; rinse under cold water. Place drained beans in medium saucepan, cover with water; bring to the boil. Reduce heat; simmer, uncovered, about 20 minutes or until tender, drain.
4 Meanwhile, heat half of the oil in medium flameproof baking dish; cook lamb, uncovered, until browned all over. Roast lamb, uncovered, in oven about 20 minutes or until cooked as desired. Cover; stand 10 minutes.
5 Meanwhile, heat remaining oil in same cleaned saucepan; cook brown onion, garlic, chilli and cumin, stirring, until onion softens. Add vinegar; cook, stirring, until liquid evaporates. Remove from heat.
6 Place onion mixture and beans in large bowl with remaining ingredients; toss gently to combine. Serve salad with sliced lamb.
preparation time 30 minutes (plus standing and refrigeration time)
cooking time 40 minutes **serves** 4
nutritional count per serving 30.2g total fat (9g saturated fat); 2353kJ (563 cal); 22.4g carbohydrate; 49.8g protein; 12.8g fibre

Gremolata-crumbed roast leg of lamb

1.7kg leg of lamb
¼ cup (60ml) lemon juice
4 cloves garlic, crushed
5 large potatoes (1.5kg)
1 medium brown onion (150g), chopped finely
2 trimmed celery stalks (200g), chopped finely
2 tablespoons plain flour
½ cup (125ml) dry red wine
2 cups (500ml) beef stock
2 sprigs fresh rosemary
1 tablespoon finely chopped fresh flat-leaf parsley
gremolata
½ cup finely chopped fresh flat-leaf parsley
1 tablespoon finely grated lemon rind
2 cloves garlic, crushed
½ cup (35g) stale breadcrumbs
1 tablespoon olive oil

1 Combine lamb with juice and half of the garlic in large bowl. Cover; refrigerate 3 hours or overnight, turning lamb occasionally in marinade.
2 Preheat oven to 180°C/160°C fan-forced.
3 Cut each potato into eight wedges. Place undrained lamb and potatoes in large flameproof baking dish; roast, uncovered, 1 hour.
4 Combine ingredients for gremolata in small bowl; press onto lamb. Roast, uncovered, further 30 minutes or until lamb is cooked as desired.
5 Remove lamb and potato from baking dish. Cover; keep warm.
6 Cook onion, celery and remaining garlic in baking dish, stirring, over heat until vegetables are soft. Stir in flour; cook, stirring, about 1 minute or until bubbling. Gradually stir in wine and stock, add rosemary; cook, stirring, until gravy thickens. Strain gravy into medium jug.
7 Serve lamb and potato wedges with gravy; sprinkle with parsley.

preparation time 15 minutes (plus refrigeration time)
cooking time 1 hour 40 minutes **serves** 6
nutritional count per serving 15.1g total fat (5.6g saturated fat); 2186kJ (523 cal); 35.6g carbohydrate; 54.3g protein; 5.3g fibre

Chilli and honey-glazed lamb loin with mee goreng

800g boned and rolled lamb loin
1 tablespoon sambal oelek
1 tablespoon honey
1 tablespoon kecap manis
mee goreng
10 dried shiitake mushrooms
450g hokkien noodles
2 teaspoons peanut oil
1cm piece fresh ginger (5g), grated
1 clove garlic, crushed
1 green onion, sliced thinly
100g snow peas, sliced thinly
1 teaspoon sambal oelek
2 tablespoons kecap manis
1 tablespoon hoisin sauce
1 tablespoon oyster sauce
⅓ cup (80ml) beef stock

1 Preheat oven to 180°C/160°C fan-forced.
2 Place lamb on oiled wire rack over baking dish; brush with combined remaining ingredients. Roast, uncovered, 30 minutes. Cover lamb; roast further 15 minutes or until cooked as desired. Cover lamb; stand 10 minutes.
3 Meanwhile, make mee goreng; serve with sliced lamb.
mee goreng place mushrooms in small heatproof bowl, cover with boiling water; stand 20 minutes or until tender, drain. Slice mushrooms thinly. Place noodles in large heatproof bowl; cover with boiling water, separate with fork, drain. Heat oil in wok; stir-fry ginger and garlic until fragrant. Add mushrooms and noodles to wok; stir-fry 2 minutes. Add remaining ingredients; stir-fry until snow peas are just tender.

preparation time 20 minutes **cooking time** 45 minutes **serves** 4
nutritional count per serving 21.5g total fat (9.1g saturated fat); 2926kJ (700 cal); 70.2g carbohydrate; 55.4g protein; 3.6g fibre

Lamb with aïoli

⅓ cup (80ml) olive oil
6 sprigs fresh thyme
900g large potatoes
6 x 4 french-trimmed cutlet lamb racks (900g)
500g spinach, trimmed
20g butter
1 clove garlic, crushed
250g swiss brown mushrooms, sliced thickly
1 tablespoon balsamic vinegar
aïoli
½ teaspoon dijon mustard
1 tablespoon white wine vinegar
1 clove garlic, crushed
2 egg yolks
¾ cup (180ml) extra virgin olive oil
2 teaspoons lemon juice

1 Heat oil in small saucepan; deep-fry thyme briefly, about 5 seconds or until fragrant. Remove thyme from oil, drain on absorbent paper; reserve oil.
2 Preheat oven to 200°C/180°C fan-forced.
3 Cut potatoes into 1cm slices. Heat 2 tablespoons of the reserved thyme oil in flameproof baking dish; cook potato slices, in batches, until lightly browned both sides. Return all potato to same baking dish.
4 Add lamb to baking dish; roast, uncovered, in oven about 15 minutes or until cooked as desired. Cover to keep warm.
5 Meanwhile, make aïoli.
6 Boil, steam or microwave spinach until just wilted; drain.
7 Heat remaining thyme oil with butter in small saucepan; cook garlic and mushrooms, stirring, until mushrooms soften.
8 Cut lamb racks into cutlets; divide among serving plates with spinach, potato and mushrooms. Top with aïoli, garnish with fried thyme; drizzle with vinegar.
aïoli whisk mustard, vinegar, garlic and egg yolks in small bowl until combined. Gradually add oil in thin, steady stream, whisking constantly, until aïoli thickens. Whisk in lemon juice.

preparation time 35 minutes **cooking time** 30 minutes **serves** 6
nutritional count per serving 51.4g total fat (11.3g saturated fat); 2700kJ (646 cal); 20.2g carbohydrate; 24.2g protein; 5.4g fibre

Roast lamb with mustard and herbs

4 medium potatoes (800g)
1 medium brown onion (150g)
1½ cups (375ml) chicken stock
1½ tablespoons dijon mustard
3 cloves garlic, crushed
2 drained anchovy fillets, chopped
2 teaspoons finely grated lemon rind
2kg leg of lamb
½ cup coarsely chopped fresh flat-leaf parsley
2 tablespoons coarsely chopped fresh oregano
1 medium lemon (140g), cut into wedges

1 Preheat oven to 180°C/160°C fan-forced.
2 Cut potatoes and onion into 1cm-thick slices. Place potato and onion in oiled baking dish; pour stock over potatoes.
3 Combine mustard, garlic, anchovies and rind in small bowl; rub all over lamb. Place lamb on top of potatoes. Roast, uncovered, about 1½ hours or until lamb is cooked as desired.
4 Remove lamb from dish; stand, covered, for 15 minutes.
5 Meanwhile, increase oven temperature to 240°C/220°C fan-forced. Bake potatoes further 15 minutes or until browned.
6 Sprinkle lamb with herbs; serve with potato mixture and lemon wedges, if desired.

preparation time 20 minutes **cooking time** 1 hour 45 minutes
serves 6
nutritional count per serving 14.0g total fat (6.1g saturated fat); 1818kJ (435 cal); 16.4g carbohydrate; 58.9g protein; 3.0g fibre

Marinated lamb leg with caponata

2kg leg of lamb
2 teaspoons sweet paprika
¼ cup (60ml) lemon juice
1 tablespoon olive oil
2 cloves garlic, crushed
3 cups (750ml) beef stock
2 teaspoons finely shredded lemon rind
2 tablespoons coarsely chopped fresh lemon thyme
caponata
2 tablespoons olive oil
6 baby eggplants (360g), chopped coarsely
2 medium brown onions (300g), chopped coarsely
3 cloves garlic, crushed
2 trimmed celery stalks (200g), chopped coarsely
2 medium red capsicums (400g), chopped coarsely
1 tablespoon drained baby capers, rinsed
2 tablespoons red wine vinegar
3 large egg tomatoes (270g), chopped coarsely
½ cup coarsely chopped fresh basil
¼ cup (40g) roasted pine nuts

1 Using sharp knife, pierce lamb all over; rub combined paprika, juice, oil and garlic over lamb, pressing into cuts. Cover; refrigerate 3 hours or overnight.
2 Preheat oven to 200°C/180°C fan-forced. Pour stock into large shallow baking dish; place lamb on oiled rack over dish, drizzle any remaining paprika mixture. Roast, uncovered, 30 minutes, brushing occasionally with pan juices. Reduce oven temperature to 180°C/160°C fan-forced; roast, uncovered, 1¼ hours or until lamb is cooked as desired. Cover lamb; stand 20 minutes.
3 Meanwhile, make caponata. Serve sliced lamb, sprinkled with combined rind and thyme, with caponata and, if desired, soft polenta.
caponata heat half of the oil in large saucepan; cook eggplant until browned. Remove from pan. Heat remaining oil in same pan; cook onion, stirring, until soft. Add garlic, celery and capsicum; cook, stirring, until vegetables soften. Stir in capers, vinegar, tomato, eggplant and half of the basil; cook, covered, over low heat about 15 minutes or until mixture thickens slightly. Stir in remaining basil and pine nuts just before serving.
preparation time 30 minutes (plus refrigeration time)
cooking time 1 hour 45 minutes (plus standing time) **serves** 4
nutritional count per serving 41.8g total fat (11.4g saturated fat); 3386kJ (810 cal); 14.9g carbohydrate; 90.2g protein; 7.3g fibre

Roast lamb with anchovies, garlic and vegetables

45g can anchovy fillets
1.5kg easy carve leg of lamb
1 tablespoon fresh rosemary leaves
2 cloves garlic, sliced thinly
2 bulbs garlic, halved horizontally, extra
4 medium parsnips (500g)
2 tablespoons olive oil
500g asparagus
12 small truss tomatoes on vine
¼ cup (60ml) red wine
1 tablespoon balsamic vinegar
1 cup (250ml) beef stock

1 Preheat oven to 180°C/160°C fan-forced. Drain anchovies over small bowl; reserve oil. Chop anchovies coarsely.
2 Using sharp knife, pierce lamb about 12 times all over, gently twisting to make a small hole. Press anchovies, rosemary and sliced garlic evenly into holes. Place lamb on oiled wire rack in baking dish; pour reserved anchovy oil over lamb. Roast, uncovered, 1 hour 20 minutes or until lamb is cooked as desired.
3 Meanwhile, place extra garlic and parsnips in separate baking dish, drizzle with half of the olive oil; roast alongside lamb 40 minutes. Add the asparagus, tomatoes and remaining olive oil; roast further 10 minutes or until vegetables are tender.
4 Remove lamb from dish. Cover; stand 10 minutes. Drain fat from dish; place dish over medium heat. Add wine; bring to the boil. Add vinegar, stock and any lamb pan juices; cook, stirring, until sauce boils and reduces to 1 cup.
5 Serve lamb with vegetables and sauce.

preparation time 25 minutes **cooking time** 1 hour 25 minutes
serves 4
nutritional count per serving 25.9g total fat (8.3g saturated fat); 2537kJ (607 cal); 16.3g carbohydrate; 70.2g protein; 8.6g fibre

Herb-crusted lamb racks with kipfler potatoes and leek

4 x 3 cutlet lamb racks (900g)
¼ cup (20g) fresh white breadcrumbs
1 tablespoon finely chopped fresh rosemary
1 tablespoon finely chopped fresh flat-leaf parsley
2 teaspoons finely chopped fresh thyme
3 cloves garlic, crushed
3 teaspoons bottled coriander pesto
1kg kipfler potatoes, halved lengthways
cooking-oil spray
1 teaspoon sea salt
2 medium leeks (700g), trimmed
20g butter
¼ cup (60ml) chicken stock
¼ cup (60ml) dry white wine

1 Preheat oven to 200°C/180°C fan-forced.
2 Remove any excess fat from lamb. Combine breadcrumbs, herbs, garlic and pesto in small bowl. Using hands, press breadcrumb mixture onto lamb racks. Cover; refrigerate until required.
3 Place potato in large shallow baking dish; spray with cooking-oil spray, sprinkle with salt. Roast, uncovered, 20 minutes. Place lamb on potato; roast, uncovered, further 10 minutes.
4 Reduce oven temperature to 150°C/130°C fan-forced; cook potato and lamb further 20 minutes or until potato is tender and lamb is cooked as desired. Remove lamb from dish. Cover; stand 5 minutes.
5 Meanwhile, cut leeks into 10cm lengths; slice thinly lengthways. Melt butter in large frying pan; cook leek, stirring, until leek softens. Stir in stock and wine; bring to the boil. Reduce heat; simmer, uncovered, until liquid reduces by half.
6 Cut racks into cutlets; serve with potato and leek.

preparation time 25 minutes (plus refrigeration time)
cooking time 55 minutes (plus standing time) **serves** 4
nutritional count per serving 26.6g total fat (12.0g saturated fat); 2328kJ (557 cal); 40.7g carbohydrate; 32.2g protein; 8.8g fibre
tip breadcrumb mixture can be patted onto racks the day before serving. Cover; refrigerate overnight.

Lamb with olive couscous seasoning

2kg leg of lamb, butterflied (ask the butcher to butterfly it for you)
1 tablespoon olive oil
⅓ cup (80ml) orange juice
½ teaspoon ground cinnamon
¼ cup (90g) honey
2 cloves garlic, crushed
1½ tablespoons cornflour
2 cups (500ml) beef stock
olive couscous seasoning
½ cup (100g) couscous
½ cup (125ml) boiling water
20g butter
1 small white onion (80g), chopped finely
1 teaspoon ground cumin
2 tablespoons flaked almonds, roasted
1 small apple (130g), peeled, cored, chopped coarsely
1 tablespoon brown sugar
¼ cup (40g) coarsely chopped black olives

1 Preheat oven to 180°C/160°C fan-forced.
2 Make olive couscous seasoning.
3 Pound lamb with meat mallet until an even thickness. Place seasoning in centre of lamb; roll up from short side to enclose seasoning. Secure lamb with skewers, tie with kitchen string at 2cm intervals. Place lamb on oiled wire rack in baking dish; brush with oil. Roast, uncovered, 1 hour.
4 Combine juice, cinnamon, honey and garlic in small bowl; brush a little juice mixture over lamb. Roast lamb further 30 minutes or until tender; bast with remaining juice mixture during cooking. Remove lamb from dish; stand, covered, 10 minutes. Remove skewers before carving.
5 Meanwhile, blend cornflour with a little of the stock in small bowl; stir into juices in baking dish with remaining stock. Stir over heat until mixture boils and thickens; strain. Serve with lamb.
olive couscous seasoning place couscous and the water in heatproof bowl; stand, covered, 5 minutes or until all the liquid has been absorbed. Meanwhile, heat butter in small frying pan, add onion; cook, stirring, until soft. Add cumin, nuts, apple, sugar and olives; cook, stirring, 3 minutes or until apple is softened slightly. Stir in couscous; cool.
preparation time 30 minutes **cooking time** 45 minutes **serves** 6
nutritional count per serving 20.2g total fat (8.3g saturated fat); 2341kJ (560 cal); 35.2g carbohydrate; 58.4g protein; 1.0g fibre

Traditional roast dinner

2kg leg of lamb
3 sprigs fresh rosemary, chopped coarsely
½ teaspoon sweet paprika
1kg potatoes, chopped coarsely
500g piece pumpkin, chopped coarsely
3 small brown onions (240g), halved
2 tablespoons olive oil
2 tablespoons plain flour
1 cup (250ml) chicken stock
¼ cup (60ml) dry red wine

1 Preheat oven to 200°C/180°C fan-forced.
2 Place lamb in large oiled baking dish; using sharp knife, score skin at 2cm intervals, sprinkle with rosemary and paprika. Roast, uncovered, 15 minutes. Reduce oven temperature to 180°C/160°C fan-forced; roast, uncovered, further 45 minutes or until cooked as desired.
3 Meanwhile, place potato, pumpkin and onion, in single layer, in large shallow baking dish; drizzle with oil. Roast, uncovered, alongside lamb for last 45 minutes of lamb cooking time. Remove lamb and vegetables from oven; cover to keep warm.
4 Strain pan juices from lamb dish into medium jug. Return ¼ cup of the pan juices to flameproof dish over medium heat, add flour; cook, stirring, 5 minutes or until mixture bubbles and browns. Gradually stir in stock and wine; cook over high heat, stirring, until gravy boils and thickens. Strain.
5 Serve sliced lamb with roasted vegetables and gravy and, if desired, cauliflower mornay.

preparation time 30 minutes **cooking time** 1 hour 10 minutes
serves 6
nutritional count per serving 20.1g total fat (7.1g saturated fat); 2316kJ (554 cal); 28.5g carbohydrate; 60.9g protein; 3.8g fibre

Slow-roasted lamb shanks

1 tablespoon olive oil
8 french-trimmed lamb shanks (about 1.2kg)
1 tablespoon sugar
1½ cups (375ml) dry red wine
2 cups (500ml) beef stock
3 cloves garlic, crushed
20g butter
1 small brown onion (80g), chopped finely
1 trimmed celery stalk (100g), chopped finely
1 tablespoon plain flour
1 tablespoon tomato paste
4 sprigs fresh rosemary, chopped coarsely
caramelised onion
40g butter
2 medium red onions (340g), sliced thinly
¼ cup (50g) brown sugar
¼ cup (60ml) raspberry vinegar

1 Preheat oven to 150°C/130°C fan-forced.
2 Heat oil in large flameproof baking dish; cook shanks over heat until browned all over. Stir in sugar, wine, stock and garlic; bring to the boil. Roast lamb, covered, in oven, about 4 hours, turning twice during cooking.
3 Meanwhile, make caramelised onion.
4 Remove lamb from dish; cover to keep warm. Pour pan juices into large heatproof jug. Return dish to heat, melt butter; cook onion and celery, stirring, until celery is just tender. Stir in flour; cook, stirring, 2 minutes. Add reserved pan juices, paste and rosemary; bring to the boil. Simmer, uncovered, stirring until it boils and thickens; strain sauce into large jug.
5 Serve lamb with sauce and caramelised onion, accompanied with pureed white beans, if desired.
caramelised onion Melt butter in medium saucepan; cook onion, stirring, about 15 minutes or until browned and soft. Stir in sugar and vinegar; cook, stirring, about 15 minutes or until onion is caramelised.

preparation time 20 minutes **cooking time** 4 hours 20 minutes
serves 4
nutritional count per serving 32.6g total fat (15.9g saturated fat); 2989kJ (715 cal); 27.1g carbohydrate; 61.6g protein; 2.5g fibre

Za'atar-rubbed lamb with chilli tabbouleh

1 tablespoon sumac
1 tablespoon toasted sesame seeds
1 teaspoon dried marjoram
1 teaspoon sweet paprika
2 teaspoons dried thyme
¼ cup (60ml) olive oil
2 mini lamb roasts (700g)
chilli tabbouleh
3 medium tomatoes (450g)
½ cup (80g) burghul
1 small red onion (100g), chopped finely
2 fresh long red chillies, sliced thinly
5 cups coarsely chopped fresh flat-leaf parsley
⅓ cup finely chopped fresh mint
½ cup (125ml) lemon juice
¼ cup (60ml) olive oil

1 Make chilli tabbouleh.
2 Preheat oven to 200°C/180°C fan-forced.
3 Combine sumac, sesame seeds, marjoram, paprika, thyme and oil in large bowl; rub lamb with za'atar mixture.
4 Place lamb on oiled wire rack in large shallow baking dish; roast, uncovered, about 25 minutes or until cooked as desired. Cover lamb, stand 5 minutes.
5 Serve sliced lamb with tabbouleh.
chilli tabbouleh chop tomatoes finely, retaining as much of the juice as possible. Place tomato and juice on top of burghul in large bowl, cover; refrigerate at least 2 hours or until burghul softens. Add remaining ingredients to large bowl; toss gently to combine.

preparation time 30 minutes (plus refrigeration time)
cooking time 25 minutes **serves** 4
nutritional count per serving 45g total fat (11.1g saturated fat); 2675kJ (640 cal); 16.2g carbohydrate; 42.5g protein; 9.1g fibre
tip za'atar, a blend of roasted dry spices, is easy to make, but a prepared mix of sesame seeds, marjoram, thyme and sumac can be purchased in Middle-Eastern food shops and delicatessens.

Greek roast lamb with skordalia and lemon-scented potatoes

2kg leg of lamb
2 cloves garlic, crushed
½ cup (125ml) lemon juice
2 tablespoons olive oil
1 tablespoon fresh oregano leaves
1 teaspoon fresh lemon thyme leaves
5 large potatoes (1.5kg), cut into 3cm pieces
2 tablespoons olive oil, extra
1 tablespoon finely grated lemon rind
2 tablespoons lemon juice
1 teaspoon fresh lemon thyme leaves
skordalia
1 medium potato (200g), quartered
3 cloves garlic, quartered
1 tablespoon lemon juice
1 tablespoon white wine vinegar
2 tablespoons water
⅓ cup (80ml) olive oil
1 tablespoon warm water

1 Combine lamb with garlic, juice, oil, oregano and thyme in large bowl. Cover; refrigerate 3 hours or overnight.
2 Preheat oven to 160°C/140°C fan-forced. Place lamb in large baking dish; roast, uncovered, 4 hours.
3 Meanwhile, make skordalia. Toss potato in large bowl with combined remaining ingredients; place, in single layer, on oven tray. Cook potato, uncovered, for last 30 minutes of lamb cooking time.
4 Remove lamb from oven; cover to keep warm. Increase oven temperature to 220°C/200°C fan-forced; roast potatoes, uncovered, 20 minutes or until crisp and tender. Serve potatoes and lamb with skordalia.
skordalia boil, steam or microwave potato until tender; drain. Push potato through food mill or fine sieve into large bowl; cool 10 minutes. Add garlic, juice, vinegar and the water to potato; stir until well combined. Place potato mixture in blender; with motor operating, gradually add oil in a thin, steady stream, only until skordalia thickens (do not overmix). Stir in the water.
preparation time 40 minutes (plus refrigeration time)
cooking time 4 hours 20 minutes (plus cooling time) **serves** 4
nutritional count per serving 57.0g total fat (14.0g saturated fat); 4556kJ (1090 cal); 51.5g carbohydrate; 91.2g protein; 6.7g fibre

Roast leg of lamb with gravy

4 sprigs fresh rosemary
2kg leg of lamb
2 cloves garlic, each cut into 8 slices
¼ cup (60ml) olive oil
40g butter
1 small brown onion (80g), chopped finely
2 tablespoons plain flour
½ cup (125ml) dry red wine
1½ cups (375ml) lamb or beef stock

1 Preheat oven to 220°C/200°C fan-forced.

2 Cut 16 similar-size rosemary sprigs from bunch; place remainder of bunch in large flameproof baking dish.

3 Remove and discard as much excess fat from lamb as possible. Using sharp knife, pierce lamb about 16 times all over; press garlic slices and rosemary sprigs into cuts. Place lamb on top of rosemary in baking dish. Pour oil over lamb; roast, uncovered, 20 minutes.

4 Reduce oven temperature to 180°C/160°C fan-forced; roast lamb, further 1½ hours, occasionally basting with pan juices. Remove lamb from dish; stand 5 minutes.

5 Drain juices from dish, melt butter in pan over low heat; cook onion, stirring, until soft. Stir in flour; cook, stirring, about 5 minutes or until browned. Pour in wine and stock; cook over high heat, stirring, until gravy boils and thickens. Strain, then serve with lamb.

preparation time 10 minutes **cooking time** 2 hours **serves** 6
nutritional count per serving 28.1g total fat (10.9g saturated fat); 2119kJ (507 cal); 3.9g carbohydrate; 56.0g protein; 0.5g fibre
tip we used red shiraz in this recipe but any dry red wine can be used.

Tamarind-glazed rack with tat soi and orange salad

You need to buy a small head of tat soi for this recipe.

¼ cup (60ml) tamarind concentrate
¼ cup (60ml) orange juice
2 teaspoons sesame oil
1 tablespoon brown sugar
4 x 4 french-trimmed cutlet racks (600g)
2 large oranges (600g)
100g tat soi leaves
100g shiitake mushrooms, sliced thickly

1 Preheat oven to 200°C/180°C fan-forced.
2 Combine tamarind, juice, oil and sugar in small saucepan; reserve 2 tablespoons of the mixture in large bowl. Bring remaining mixture in pan to the boil. Reduce heat; simmer, uncovered, about 2 minutes or until mixture thickens slightly.
3 Place lamb on oiled wire rack inside large shallow baking dish; brush hot tamarind glaze over racks. Roast, uncovered, about 20 minutes or until racks are cooked as desired. Cover racks; stand 10 minutes.
4 Meanwhile, segment oranges over reserved tamarind mixture in bowl. Add tat soi and mushrooms; toss gently to combine.
5 Cut each lamb rack in half; place two halves on each serving plate, serve with salad.

preparation time 10 minutes **cooking time** 25 minutes **serves** 4
nutritional count per serving 15.4g total fat (6.2g saturated fat); 1132kJ (271 cal); 15.7g carbohydrate; 17.7g protein; 3.4g fibre

Parmesan and gremolata lamb racks with parsley and chilli risotto

½ cup coarsely chopped fresh flat-leaf parsley
1 tablespoon finely grated lemon rind
⅓ cup (25g) finely grated parmesan cheese
3 cloves garlic, crushed
1 tablespoon olive oil
2 x 8 french-trimmed cutlet lamb racks (600g)
parsley and chilli risotto
3 cups (750ml) chicken stock
3 cups (750ml) water
1 tablespoon olive oil
1 medium brown onion (150g), chopped coarsely
1½ cups (300g) arborio rice
½ cup (125ml) dry white wine
1 teaspoon finely grated lemon rind
1 fresh small red thai chilli, chopped finely
½ cup (40g) finely grated parmesan cheese
2 cups loosely packed fresh flat-leaf parsley leaves

1 Preheat oven to 200°C/180°C fan-forced.
2 Combine parsley, rind, cheese, garlic and oil in small bowl. Place lamb in large shallow oiled baking dish; press gremolata mixture onto fatty side of each rack. Roast, uncovered, 30 minutes or until lamb is cooked as desired.
3 Meanwhile, make parsley and chilli risotto.
4 Cut each lamb rack in half; serve with risotto.
parsley and chilli risotto bring stock and the water to the boil in medium saucepan. Reduce heat; simmer, covered. Heat oil in large saucepan; cook onion, stirring, 5 minutes or until onion softens. Add rice; stir to coat in mixture. Add wine; cook, stirring, until liquid is absorbed. Stir in 1 cup simmering stock mixture; cook, stirring, over low heat until liquid is absorbed. Continue adding stock mixture, in 1-cup batches, stirring, until liquid is almost absorbed after each addition. Total cooking time should be about 35 minutes or until rice is tender. Just before serving, stir in rind, chilli, cheese and parsley.

preparation time 30 minutes **cooking time** 40 minutes **serves** 4
nutritional count per serving 28.5g total fat (11g saturated fat); 2713kJ (649 cal); 63.3g carbohydrate; 29.7g protein; 3.1g fibre

Roast lamb with green onions, potatoes and garlic

24 green onions, trimmed to 10cm lengths
2kg medium potatoes
¾ cup (180ml) extra virgin olive oil
2 cloves garlic, crushed
15 sprigs thyme, chopped coarsely
2 bay leaves
6 black peppercorns
2 boned legs of lamb (1.6kg)
40 whole garlic cloves, peeled
¼ cup (60ml) balsamic vinegar
2 cups (240g) seeded black olives

1 Slice one end of onions, lengthways, to halfway; stand, cut-end down, in small jug water. Refrigerate 1 hour or until onions separate and curl slightly.
2 Preheat oven to 240°C/220°C fan-forced. Cut potatoes into 3cm cubes; combine with 2 tablespoons of the oil, in single layer, in large shallow baking dish. Roast, uncovered, 1 hour or until tender, stirring occasionally. Remove potato from oven; reserve in dish.
3 Reduce oven temperature to 150°C/130°C fan-forced. Combine crushed garlic, thyme, bay leaves and peppercorns in small bowl. Place lamb on board, cut-side up; cover with plastic wrap, pound with meat mallet then rub cut-side of lamb with garlic mixture. Roll each leg tightly; tie with kitchen string at 2cm intervals. Place lamb in large deep baking dish, brush with 2 tablespoons of the oil; roast, uncovered, 40 minutes.
4 Meanwhile, place whole garlic cloves in small baking dish, sprinkle with 2 tablespoons of the oil; roast, uncovered, alongside lamb, 20 minutes.
5 Dry onions with absorbent paper. Combine remaining oil and vinegar in small jug. Place onions, cut-end down, in vinegar mixture; reserve.
6 When lamb is cooked as desired and garlic just tender, remove from oven. Cover lamb with foil to keep warm.
7 Increase oven temperature to 200°C/180°C fan-forced. Add garlic and olives to potato in baking dish; heat, uncovered, in oven 5 minutes.
8 Cut lamb into eight rounds. Divide potatoes among serving plates; top with lamb and green onions. Drizzle with remaining vinegar mixture.
preparation time 40 minutes (plus refrigeration time)
cooking time 1 hour 40 minutes (plus standing time) **serves** 8
nutritional count per serving 32.3g total fat (7.9g saturated fat); 2717kJ (650 cal); 35.9g carbohydrate; 50.7g protein; 6.9g fibre

Slow-cooked thai lamb shanks

2 star anise
2 teaspoons ground coriander
⅓ cup (100g) tamarind concentrate
2 tablespoons brown sugar
8cm piece fresh ginger (40g), sliced thinly
1 fresh small red thai chilli, sliced thinly
2 cloves garlic, sliced thinly
1 tablespoon kecap manis
1 cup (250ml) water
8 french-trimmed lamb shanks (2kg)
500g choy sum, chopped into 10cm lengths

1 Preheat oven to 180°C/160°C fan-forced.
2 Dry-fry star anise and coriander in small heated frying pan, stirring, until fragrant. Combine spices with tamarind, sugar, ginger, chilli, garlic, kecap manis and the water in medium jug.
3 Place lamb, in single layer, in large shallow baking dish; drizzle with tamarind mixture. Roast, covered, turning lamb occasionally, 2 hours or until meat is almost falling off the bone. Remove lamb from dish; cover to keep warm.
4 Skim away excess fat from lamb pan juices then strain into small saucepan. Bring sauce to the boil; boil, uncovered, 5 minutes.
5 Steam choy sum until just tender then divide among serving plates. Top with lamb; drizzle with sauce.

preparation time 30 minutes **cooking time** 2 hours 15 minutes
serves 4
nutritional count per serving 12.5g total fat (5.6g saturated fat); 1492kJ (357 cal); 11.7g carbohydrate; 48.1g protein; 2.6g fibre

Slow-roasted lamb leg with artichokes and lemon

½ cup coarsely chopped fresh flat-leaf parsley
½ cup (75g) seeded kalamata olives, quartered
4 drained anchovy fillets
4 cloves garlic, quartered
2 teaspoons finely grated lemon rind
2 tablespoons lemon juice
2 tablespoons drained capers, rinsed
2 tablespoons olive oil
2kg leg of lamb
800g jerusalem artichokes, halved lengthways
2 small red onions (200g), cut into wedges
2 medium lemons (280g), cut into wedges
12 cloves garlic, unpeeled

1 Preheat oven to 150°C/130°C fan-forced.
2 Blend or process parsley, olives, anchovies, quartered garlic, rind, juice, capers and 1 tablespoon of the oil until mixture is chopped coarsely.
3 Using sharp knife, pierce lamb down to the bone at 3cm intervals along the length of the leg. Spread olive mixture all over lamb, pressing into cuts.
4 Combine artichokes, onion, lemon, unpeeled garlic and remaining oil in large shallow baking dish. Place lamb on artichoke mixture; cover tightly with foil. Roast, uncovered, 4 hours.
5 Serve lamb with vegetable mixture.

preparation time 30 minutes **cooking time** 4 hours **serves** 4
nutritional count per serving 30.4g total fat (10.4g saturated fat);
2888kJ (691 cal); 14.6g carbohydrate; 87.8g protein; 8.7g fibre

Raan with coriander yogurt

2 teaspoons coriander seeds
1 teaspoon cumin seeds
5 cardamom pods, bruised
1 teaspoon chilli powder
1 teaspoon ground turmeric
1 cinnamon stick
2 cloves
2 star anise
1 medium brown onion (150g), chopped coarsely
4 cloves garlic, peeled
2cm piece fresh ginger (10g), grated finely
¼ cup (40g) blanched almonds
½ cup (140g) yogurt
2 tablespoons lemon juice
2kg leg of lamb, trimmed
coriander yogurt
1 cup (280g) yogurt
¼ cup coarsely chopped fresh coriander

1 Dry-fry seeds, cardamom, chilli, turmeric, cinnamon, cloves and star anise in heated small frying pan, stirring, about 2 minutes or until fragrant. Blend or process spices with onion, garlic, ginger, nuts, yogurt and juice until mixture forms a paste.
2 Using sharp knife, pierce lamb all over; place on oiled wire rack in large shallow baking dish. Spread paste over lamb, pressing firmly into cuts. Cover; refrigerate overnight.
3 Preheat oven to 200°C/180°C fan-forced.
4 Remove lamb from refrigerator; pour enough water into baking dish to completely cover base. Cover dish with foil; roast lamb 30 minutes. Reduce oven temperature to 150°C/130°C fan-forced; roast lamb, covered, further 1½ hours. Uncover; roast about 30 minutes or until lamb is cooked as desired. Cover lamb; stand 10 minutes.
5 Meanwhile, combine ingredients for coriander yogurt.
6 Serve sliced lamb with yogurt and, if desired, pilaf.

preparation time 15 minutes (plus refrigeration time)
cooking time 2 hours 35 minutes **serves** 6
nutritional count per serving 19.5g total fat (7.7g saturated fat); 1831kJ (438 cal); 5.0g carbohydrate; 59.8g protein; 1.4g fibre

Port and balsamic slow-roasted lamb

2.5kg leg of lamb
¼ cup (30g) sea salt flakes
20g butter
1 tablespoon olive oil
⅓ cup (80ml) dry red wine
⅓ cup (80ml) balsamic vinegar
⅓ cup (80ml) port
¼ cup (60ml) beef stock
8 cloves garlic, crushed
8 medium egg tomatoes (600g), halved lengthways

1 Preheat oven to 120°C/100°C fan-forced.
2 Bring a large saucepan of water to the boil; add lamb, simmer
15 minutes. Drain; pat lamb dry. Using sharp knife, pierce lamb all over;
press salt into cuts.
3 Heat butter and oil in large flameproof dish; cook lamb, turning, until
browned all over. Add wine, vinegar, port, stock and garlic to dish; roast
lamb, covered, in oven 4½ hours.
4 Add tomatoes, cut-side up, to dish; roast further 2 hours, uncovered,
basting occasionally.
5 Remove lamb and tomatoes from dish; boil pan juices over heat until
reduced by half. Serve with lamb and tomatoes.

preparation time 15 minutes **cooking time** 6 hours 55 minutes
serves 6
nutritional count per serving 22.7g total fat (9.7g saturated fat);
2186kJ (52 cal); 4.5g carbohydrate; 69.6g protein; 2.1g fibre

pork

Crisp five-spice salt pork belly

Ask your butcher to score the rind diagonally at 5mm intervals.

1kg piece boneless pork belly, rind on
1½ teaspoons fine sea salt (not salt flakes)
½ teaspoon five-spice powder
1 tablespoon peanut oil
¼ cup (60ml) light soy sauce
1 fresh small red thai chilli, chopped finely

1 Pat pork rind dry with absorbent paper; rub with combined salt, five-spice and oil. Place pork on oiled wire rack over large shallow baking dish; cover, refrigerate 1 hour.
2 Preheat oven to 240°C/220°C fan-forced.
3 Roast pork, uncovered, 1 hour or until rind begins to crisp.
4 Reduce oven temperature to 170°C/150°C fan-forced; roast pork further 30 minutes or until tender. Stand, uncovered, 15 minutes.
5 Cut pork into thick slices; serve with combined soy sauce and chilli.

preparation time 15 minutes (plus refrigeration time)
cooking time 1 hour 30 minutes **serves** 8 as part of a banquet
nutritional count per serving 30.2g total fat (9.9g saturated fat); 1509kJ (361 cal); 0.2g carbohydrate; 23.1g protein; 0.0g fibre

Barbecue spareribs

Ask your butcher to cut pork spareribs "American-style" for this recipe.
Trimmed of almost all fat, the meat usually comes in racks of 8 to 10 ribs.

3.5kg american-style pork spareribs
barbecue sauce
2¼ cups (560ml) tomato sauce
1½ cups (375ml) cider vinegar
⅓ cup (80ml) olive oil
½ cup (125ml) worcestershire sauce
¾ cup (165g) firmly packed brown sugar
⅓ cup (95g) american-style mustard
1½ teaspoons cracked black pepper
3 fresh small red thai chillies, chopped finely
3 cloves garlic, crushed
¼ cup (60ml) lemon juice

1 Make barbecue sauce.
2 Brush both sides of ribs with barbecue sauce; place in large deep
baking dish. Pour remaining sauce over ribs, cover; refrigerate overnight,
turning ribs occasionally in the sauce.
3 Preheat oven to 160°C/140°C fan-forced.
4 Drain ribs; reserve sauce. Divide ribs between two wire racks over two
large shallow baking dishes. Roast, covered, 1½ hours; brush with sauce
every 20 minutes. Turn ribs midway through cooking time.
5 Increase oven temperature to 220°C/200°C fan-forced. Uncover ribs;
roast, brushing frequently with sauce, until ribs are browned and cooked
through, turning after 15 minutes.
6 Place remaining barbecue sauce in small saucepan; bring to the boil.
Reduce heat; simmer, stirring, about 4 minutes or until sauce thickens
slightly. Using scissors, cut ribs in portions of two or three ribs; serve ribs
with hot sauce.
barbecue sauce bring ingredients to the boil in medium saucepan.
Remove from heat; cool.

preparation time 25 minutes (plus refrigeration time)
cooking time 2 hours 10 minutes **serves** 8
nutritional count per serving 12.9g total fat (2.3g saturated fat);
1998kJ (478 cal); 42.1g carbohydrate; 46.5g protein; 2.2g fibre

Roast rolled pork loin and crackling

2.5kg boneless loin of pork, rind on
1 tablespoon olive oil
2 teaspoons fine sea salt
1 tablespoon plain flour
1½ cups (375ml) chicken stock
apricot, prune and rice stuffing
⅔ cup (130g) white long-grain rice
½ cup (75g) finely chopped dried apricots
½ cup (105g) finely chopped prunes

1 Preheat oven to 240°C/220°C fan-forced.
2 Place pork on board, rind-side up. Run a sharp knife about 5mm under rind, between it and the meat, gradually lifting and easing rind away from pork. Place rind, right-side up, in large shallow flameproof baking dish. Score rind, making diagonal cuts; rub with half of the oil, sprinkle with salt. Roast, uncovered, about 40 minutes or until crackling is well browned and crisp. Chop crackling into serving pieces. Reduce oven temperature to 220°C/200°C fan-forced.
3 Meanwhile, make apricot, prune and rice stuffing.
4 Place pork, fat-side down, on board. Slice through the thickest part of the meat horizontally, without cutting through at the side. Open out meat to form one large piece; press stuffing against the loin along width. Roll pork to enclose stuffing; secure with kitchen string at 2cm intervals.
5 Return pork to same dish, brush with remaining oil; roast, uncovered, 1 hour or until cooked through. Remove from dish; cover to keep warm.
6 Pour pan juices from pork dish into medium jug. Add 1 tablespoon of the pan juices to pork dish over medium heat, stir in flour; cook, stirring, until mixture bubbles and is browned to your liking. Gradually add remaining pan juices and stock; cook, stirring, until gravy boils and thickens. Pour gravy into serving jug.
7 Serve pork with gravy and reheated crackling.
apricot, prune and rice stuffing cook rice in large saucepan of boiling water, uncovered, 15 minutes or until just tender; drain. Combine cooled rice in large bowl with remaining ingredients.
preparation time 30 minutes
cooking time 2 hours (plus cooling time) **serves** 6
nutritional count per serving 96.4g total fat (32.2g saturated fat); 5426kJ (1298 cal); 29.8g carbohydrate; 78.7g protein; 2.7g fibre

Pork loin with fresh peach chutney

2kg boneless loin of pork, rind on
1 tablespoon olive oil
½ teaspoon celery seeds
1 teaspoon fine sea salt
fresh peach chutney
2 large peaches (440g), chopped coarsely
1 large brown onion (200g), chopped coarsely
¼ cup (40g) coarsely chopped raisins
1cm piece fresh ginger (5g), grated
1 cup (220g) white sugar
1 cup (250ml) cider vinegar
1 cinnamon stick
¼ teaspoon ground clove

1 Make fresh peach chutney.
2 Preheat oven to 200°C/180°C fan-forced.
3 Remove rind from loin; reserve. Rub pork with half of the oil; sprinkle with seeds. Place pork on oiled wire rack in large baking dish; roast, uncovered, about 1 hour or until cooked through. Remove from oven; place pork on board, cover to keep warm.
4 Increase oven temperature to 220°C/200°C fan-forced.
5 Remove excess fat from underside of reserved rind; score rind, rub with remaining oil and salt. Place rind, fatty-side up, on oiled wire rack in same baking dish; roast, uncovered, about 15 minutes or until crisp and browned. Drain on absorbent paper.
6 Serve thickly sliced pork and crackling with chutney and, if desired, salad.
fresh peach chutney stir ingredients in medium saucepan over heat, without boiling, until sugar dissolves; bring to the boil. Reduce heat; simmer, uncovered, stirring occasionally, 1¾ hours or until mixture thickens.

preparation time 35 minutes **cooking time** 3 hours **serves** 6
nutritional count per serving 8.5g total fat (2.1g saturated fat); 2429kJ (581 cal); 47.1g carbohydrate; 76.6g protein; 1.7g fibre
tip the chutney can be made up to a week ahead. Place in a sterilised jar while still hot; seal, cool, then refrigerate until required.

Roast pork with garlic and rosemary

1.5kg pork neck
3 cloves garlic, crushed
1 tablespoon chopped fresh rosemary
1 tablespoon coarse cooking salt
2 tablespoons olive oil
3 bay leaves
1 cup (250ml) water
⅓ cup (80ml) red wine vinegar

1 Preheat oven to 200°C/180°C fan-forced.
2 Tie pork with kitchen string at 3cm intervals.
3 Combine garlic, rosemary, salt and oil in small bowl; rub mixture over pork. Place pork on wire rack in baking dish; add bay leaves, the water and vinegar to dish.
4 Roast pork about 1½ hours or until cooked through. Cover pork; stand 10 minutes before slicing.

preparation time 20 minutes
cooking time 1 hour 30 minutes (plus standing time) **serves** 6
nutritional count per serving 26.1g total fat (7.6g saturated fat); 1877kJ (449 cal); 0.2g carbohydrate; 53.1g protein; 0.3g fibre

Pork fillet with apple and leek

800g pork fillets
¾ cup (180ml) chicken stock
2 medium leeks (700g), sliced thickly
1 clove garlic, crushed
2 tablespoons brown sugar
2 tablespoons red wine vinegar
2 medium apples (300g)
10g butter
1 tablespoon brown sugar, extra
400g baby carrots, trimmed, halved
8 medium patty-pan squash (100g), quartered
250g asparagus, trimmed, chopped coarsely

1 Preheat oven to 240°C/220°C fan-forced.
2 Place pork, in single layer, in large baking dish; roast, uncovered, about 25 minutes or until pork is browned and cooked through. Cover; stand 5 minutes before slicing thickly.
3 Meanwhile, heat half of the stock in medium frying pan; cook leek and garlic, stirring, until leek softens and browns slightly. Add sugar and vinegar; cook, stirring, about 5 minutes or until leek caramelises. Add remaining stock; bring to the boil. Reduce heat; simmer, uncovered, about 5 minutes or until liquid reduces by half. Place leek mixture in medium bowl; cover to keep warm.
4 Peel, core and halve apples; cut into thick slices. Melt butter in same pan; cook apple and extra sugar, stirring, until apple is browned and tender.
5 Boil, steam or microwave carrot, squash and asparagus, separately, until just tender; drain.
6 Divide mixed vegetables among serving plates, top with pork, sweet and sour leek, then apple.

preparation time 10 minutes **cooking time** 25 minutes **serves** 4
nutritional count per serving 6.1g total fat (2.4g saturated fat); 1605kJ (384 cal); 26.5g carbohydrate; 51.0g protein; 8.3g fibre
tip sweet and sour leek can be made several hours ahead; just reheat before serving.

Roasted pork belly with plum sauce

800g boneless pork belly, rind on
2 teaspoons fine sea salt
1 teaspoon olive oil
1 cup (250ml) water
1½ cups (375ml) chicken stock
2 tablespoons soy sauce
¼ cup (60ml) chinese cooking wine
¼ cup (55g) firmly packed brown sugar
2 cloves garlic, sliced thinly
3cm piece fresh ginger (15g), sliced thinly
1 cinnamon stick, crushed
1 teaspoon dried chilli flakes
⅓ cup (80ml) orange juice
6 whole cloves
1 teaspoon fennel seeds
4 plums (450g), cut into eight wedges
cucumber salad
1 lebanese cucumber (130g)
1 fresh long green chilli, sliced thinly
⅔ cup coarsely chopped fresh mint
1 tablespoon olive oil
1 tablespoon lemon juice
1 teaspoon caster sugar

1 Preheat oven to 180°C/160°C fan-forced. Place pork on board, rind-side up. Using sharp knife, score rind by making shallow cuts diagonally in both directions at 3cm intervals; rub combined salt and oil into cuts.
2 Combine the water, stock, soy sauce, wine, sugar, garlic, ginger, cinnamon, chilli, juice, cloves and seeds in large shallow baking dish. Place pork in dish, rind-side up; roast, uncovered, 1 hour 20 minutes. Increase oven temperature to 240°C/220°C fan-forced. Roast pork, uncovered, further 15 minutes or until crackling is crisp. Remove pork from dish; cover to keep warm.
3 Strain pan juices from dish into saucepan, skim away surface fat; bring to the boil. Add plums; simmer, uncovered, 15 minutes or until thickened.
4 Meanwhile, make cucumber salad; serve with sliced pork and sauce.
cucumber salad using vegetable peeler, cut cucumber lengthways into ribbons. Place in large bowl with remaining ingredients; toss to combine.
preparation time 20 minutes **cooking time** 1 hour 55 minutes **serves** 4
nutritional count per serving 51.0g total fat (16.2g saturated fat); 3010kJ (720 cal); 25.6g carbohydrate; 39.1g protein; 3.4g fibre

Chinese roast pork neck

2kg piece pork neck
¼ cup (60ml) soy sauce
2 tablespoons dry sherry
1 tablespoon brown sugar
1 tablespoon honey
1 teaspoon red food colouring
1 clove garlic, crushed
½ teaspoon five-spice powder

1 Halve pork lengthways. Combine pork in large bowl with remaining ingredients. Cover; refrigerate 3 hours or overnight.
2 Preheat oven to 220°C/200°C fan-forced.
3 Drain pork; reserve marinade. Place pork on oiled wire rack in baking dish; roast, uncovered, 30 minutes. Reduce oven temperature to 180°C/160°C fan-forced; roast, uncovered, further 1 hour or until pork is browned and cooked through, brushing occasionally with reserved marinade. Stand pork, covered, 10 minutes before slicing.

preparation time 10 minutes (plus refrigeration time)
cooking time 1 hour 30 minutes (plus standing time) **serves** 6
nutritional count per serving 5.3g total fat (1.7g saturated fat); 1622kJ (388 cal); 6.4g carbohydrate; 75.9g protein; 0.1g fibre

Lemon and garlic rack of pork

Ask your butcher to score the rind of the pork diagonally.

2 tablespoons finely grated lemon rind
3 cloves garlic, crushed
1 teaspoon cracked black pepper
1 tablespoon olive oil
2.6kg full rack of pork
6 fresh bay leaves
1 tablespoon olive oil, extra
2 teaspoons cooking salt
½ cup (125ml) dry white wine
2½ cups (625ml) chicken stock
2 teaspoons cornflour
1 tablespoon water

1 Preheat oven to 240°C/220°C fan-forced.
2 Combine lemon rind, garlic, pepper and oil in small bowl; rub underside of rack. Place bay leaves on oiled wire rack in large shallow flameproof baking dish; top with pork.
3 Rub pork rind with extra oil; sprinkle with salt. Roast, uncovered, about 30 minutes or until rind blisters. Reduce oven temperature to 180°C/160°C fan-forced; roast further 1 hour 15 minutes or until pork is just cooked through. Remove pork from dish; cover to keep warm.
4 Drain excess fat from baking dish. Place dish over heat, add wine; cook, stirring, until wine is reduced by half. Add stock; bring to the boil. Stir in blended cornflour and water; cook, stirring, until mixture boils and thickens. Strain into serving jug.
5 Serve pork with sauce.

preparation time 20 minutes **cooking time** 2 hours **serves** 10
nutritional count per serving 50.0g total fat (16.4g saturated fat); 2353kJ (563 cal); 1.1g carbohydrate; 26.8g protein; 0.2g fibre

Apple-stuffed pork loin

2.5kg boneless pork loin with 20cm flap
2 tablespoons coarse cooking salt
3 cups (750ml) sparkling apple cider
½ cup (125ml) chicken stock
3 teaspoons white sugar
apple stuffing
30g butter
3 large granny smith apples (600g), peeled, cored, cut into thin wedges
1 medium leek (350g), sliced thinly
1 medium brown onion (150g), sliced thinly
½ teaspoon ground cinnamon
2 tablespoons white sugar
1 cup (70g) stale breadcrumbs
1 tablespoon finely grated lemon rind
1 cup coarsely chopped fresh flat-leaf parsley

1 Preheat oven to 240°C/220°C fan-forced.
2 Place pork on board, rind-side up. Run sharp knife about 5mm under rind, gradually lifting rind away; place rind in large shallow baking dish. Using sharp knife, score rind at 3cm intervals forming diamonds; rub with salt. Roast, uncovered, 30 minutes or until crackling is browned and crisp. Chop crackling into serving pieces; reserve.
3 Reduce oven temperature to 180°C/160°C fan-forced.
4 Meanwhile, make apple stuffing.
5 Slice through the thickest part of pork horizontally, without cutting all the way through. Open pork out to form one large piece; press stuffing against the loin along length of pork. Roll pork to enclose stuffing; secure with kitchen string at 2cm intervals.
6 Place pork on wire rack in large shallow flameproof baking dish; pour 2½ cups of the cider into dish. Roast, uncovered, about 1½ hours or until cooked through. Remove pork from baking dish; cover to keep warm.
7 Place baking dish over heat, add stock, sugar and remaining cider; cook, stirring, until sauce thickens slightly.
8 Serve pork and crackling with sauce and, if desired, braised red cabbage.
apple stuffing heat butter in large frying pan; cook apple, leek, onion, cinnamon and sugar, stirring, until leek and onion soften. Remove from heat; stir in breadcrumbs, rind and parsley.
preparation time 1 hour **cooking time** 2 hours 15 minutes **serves** 8
nutritional count per serving 23.9g total fat (9.2g saturated fat); 2387kJ (571 cal); 27.6g carbohydrate; 59.6g protein; 2.9g fibre

Leg of pork with apple and onion compote

4kg leg of pork
2 tablespoons fresh sage leaves
2 cloves garlic, sliced thinly
1 tablespoon olive oil
2 tablespoons salt
1 teaspoon fennel seeds
apple and onion compote
40g butter
3 large brown onions (600g), sliced thinly
2 tablespoons sugar
¼ cup (60ml) cider vinegar
¾ cup (180ml) water
4 large apples (180g), peeled, sliced

1 Preheat oven to 240°C/220°C fan-forced.
2 Using sharp knife, pierce pork about 12 times all over, gently twisting to make a small hole. Press sage and sliced garlic evenly into holes.
3 Rub rind with oil and salt, rub underside of the pork with fennel seeds. Place pork on oiled wire rack in baking dish. Roast, uncovered, 30 minutes or until rind blisters. Reduce oven temperature to 180°C/160°C fan-forced; roast further 2½ hours or until cooked through.
4 Meanwhile, make apple and onion compote.
5 Serve pork with compote and steamed green beans, if desired.
apple and onion compote heat butter in large frying pan; cook onion, stirring occasionally, about 10 minutes. Add sugar; cook, stirring occasionally about 10 minutes or until onion caramelises. Stir in vinegar, water and apples; bring to the boil. Reduce heat; simmer, covered about 15 minutes or until apples are soft.

preparation time 30 minutes **cooking time** 3 hours **serves** 10
nutritional count per serving 28.6g total fat (10.4g saturated fat); 2437kJ (583 cal); 14.6g carbohydrate; 65.6g protein; 2.1g fibre

Sticky pork with kumara

This recipe is best made close to serving.

1kg kumara
2 tablespoons peanut oil
¼ cup (60ml) char siu sauce
1 tablespoon honey
2cm piece fresh ginger (10g), grated
1kg pork fillets
⅓ cup (80ml) water
¾ cup (180ml) chicken stock

1 Preheat oven to 220°C/200°C fan-forced.
2 Peel kumara, then slice into 2cm rounds. Combine kumara and oil in large shallow baking dish. Roast, uncovered, 20 minutes, turning once.
3 Combine sauce, honey and ginger in small bowl. Place pork on oiled wire rack in separate baking dish; brush pork all over with sauce mixture. Pour the water into dish.
4 Roast pork and kumara, uncovered, 20 minutes, brushing pork with its pan juices twice during cooking until cooked through. Remove pork from dish; brush with pan juices. Cover with foil; stand 5 minutes before serving.
5 Place pork baking dish over heat, add stock; bring to the boil. Strain.
6 Serve pork and kumara with pan juices and chives, if desired.

preparation time 10 minutes
cooking time 30 minutes (plus standing time) **serves** 4
nutritional count per serving 30.4g total fat (8.6g saturated fat); 2867kJ (686 cal); 42.3g carbohydrate; 57.9g protein; 5.6g fibre

Asian-style baked ham

8kg cooked leg of ham
1 cup (250ml) soy sauce
¾ cup (180ml) dry sherry
⅓ cup (75g) firmly packed brown sugar
⅓ cup (120g) honey
2 teaspoons red food colouring
4 cloves garlic, crushed
2 teaspoons five-spice powder
60 cloves (approximately)

1 Cut through rind about 10cm from shank end of leg in decorative
pattern; run thumb around edge of rind just under skin to remove rind.
Start pulling rind from shank end to widest edge of ham; discard rind.
2 Using sharp knife, make shallow cuts in one direction diagonally
across fat at 3cm intervals, then shallow-cut in opposite direction, forming
diamonds. Do not cut through top fat or fat will spread apart during cooking.
3 Combine soy sauce, sherry, sugar, honey, colouring, garlic and five-spice
in small bowl. Place ham on oiled wire rack in large baking dish; brush
with soy mixture. Push a clove in centre of each diamond shape. Cover;
refrigerate overnight.
4 Preheat oven to 180°C/160°C fan-forced.
5 Place ham on wire rack in large baking dish; pour soy mixture into
small jug. Cover ham with greased foil; roast 1 hour. Uncover; roast
further 30 minutes or until ham is lightly caramelised, brushing frequently
with soy mixture during cooking.

preparation time 15 minutes (plus refrigeration time)
cooking time 1 hour 30 minutes **serves** 10
nutritional count per serving 39.4g total fat (13.5g saturated fat);
3444kJ (824 cal); 18.2g carbohydrate; 94.3g protein; 8.2g fibre
tip as an alternative to the Asian flavours used above, a glaze of orange,
ginger and maple syrup also goes beautifully with this ham. Combine
1 cup maple syrup, 1 cup fresh orange juice, ⅓ cup orange marmalade,
¼ cup grated fresh ginger and 2 teaspoons finely grated orange rind
in small saucepan; bring to the boil. Reduce heat; simmer, uncovered,
15 minutes then strain before brushing over ham during baking.

Honey sesame ribs

4 racks american-style pork spareribs (1.5kg)
honey sesame marinade
¼ cup (90g) honey
½ cup (125ml) kecap manis
2 teaspoons sesame oil
2 star anise
1 tablespoon sesame seeds, toasted
2cm piece fresh ginger (10g), grated
1 clove garlic, crushed

1 Combine ingredients for honey sesame marinade in small bowl.
2 Place pork in large shallow dish; add two-thirds of the marinade.
Cover; refrigerate 3 hours or overnight, turning occasionally.
3 Preheat oven to 160°C/140°C fan-forced. Line two baking dishes
with baking paper or foil; place oiled wire rack in each dish.
4 Drain pork from marinade. Place pork, in single layer, on racks in
dishes. Roast, uncovered, 45 minutes, turning halfway and brushing
with remaining marinade until well browned and cooked through.

preparation time 20 minutes (plus refrigeration time)
cooking time 45 minutes **serves** 6
nutritional count per serving 11.6g total fat (3.4g saturated fat);
1083kJ (259 cal); 13.0g carbohydrate; 25.5g protein; 0.3g fibre

Asian-spiced roasted pork belly

1kg boneless pork belly, skin on
½ cup (125ml) chinese cooking wine
¼ cup (60ml) soy sauce
1 tablespoon tamarind concentrate
2 tablespoons honey
½ teaspoon sesame oil
4cm piece fresh ginger (20g), chopped finely
3 cloves garlic, crushed
2 teaspoons five-spice powder
1 star anise
1 dried long red chilli
1 teaspoon sichuan pepper
3 cups (750ml) water
900g baby buk choy, halved lengthways

1 Place pork in large saucepan of boiling water; return to the boil. Reduce heat; simmer, uncovered, about 40 minutes or until pork is cooked through, drain.
2 Combine pork in large bowl with wine, soy sauce, tamarind, honey, oil, ginger, garlic, five-spice, star anise, chilli, pepper and the water. Cover; refrigerate 3 hours or overnight.
3 Preheat oven to 220°C/200°C fan-forced.
4 Place pork, skin-side up, on oiled wire rack in large shallow baking dish; reserve marinade. Pour enough water into baking dish to come halfway up side of dish. Roast pork, uncovered, 30 minutes or until browned.
5 Meanwhile, strain marinade into small saucepan; bring to the boil. Boil, uncovered, 20 minutes or until reduced to about 1 cup. Boil, steam or microwave buk choy until just tender; drain.
6 Serve pork with sauce and buk choy.

preparation time 10 minutes (plus refrigeration time)
cooking time 1 hour 25 minutes **serves** 6
nutritional count per serving 37.9g total fat (12.7g saturated fat); 2195kJ (525 cal); 10.3g carbohydrate; 32.6g protein; 2.4g fibre

Glazed ham with mango and chilli salsa

8kg cooked leg of ham
⅔ cup (230g) mango chutney
2 tablespoons brown sugar
2½ cups (625ml) water
14 fresh long red chillies
mango and chilli salsa
2 medium mangoes (850g), chopped coarsely
2 tablespoons mango chutney
½ small red onion (50g), chopped finely
1 tablespoon lime juice

1 Preheat oven to 180°C/160°C fan-forced.
2 Cut through rind 10cm from shank end of leg; run thumb around edge of rind just under skin to remove rind. Start pulling rind from shank end to widest edge of ham; discard rind. (Reserved rind can be used to cover the cut surface of ham to keep it moist during storage.)
3 Using sharp knife, score fat by making shallow cuts diagonally in both directions at 4cm intervals.
4 For glaze, stir chutney, sugar and ¼ cup (60ml) of the water in small saucepan over low heat until sugar is dissolved.
5 Place ham on oiled wire rack in large baking dish; pour remaining water into dish. Brush ham all over with glaze; cover shank end with foil. Roast, uncovered, 50 minutes, brushing occasionally with glaze during cooking. Scatter chillies around ham in dish; roast further 30 minutes or until chillies are browned lightly and tender, and ham is browned as desired.
6 Make mango and chilli salsa.
7 Slice some of the remaining baked chillies coarsely and sprinkle over ham.
8 Serve ham with salsa and remaining baked chillies.
mango and chilli salsa seed and chop four of the baked chillies. Combine chopped chillies in medium bowl with mango, chutney, onion and juice to taste.

preparation time 30 minutes **cooking time** 1 hour 20 minutes
serves 10
nutritional count per serving 34.0g total fat (12.4g saturated fat); 3507kJ (839 cal); 22.6g carbohydrate; 109.2g protein; 1.7g fibre

Honey-glazed pork with sage

Ask your butcher to remove the rind completely from the pork loin
and score it.

2.5kg boneless loin of pork
2 teaspoons vegetable oil
1 tablespoon fine sea salt
2 cloves garlic, crushed
1 tablespoon finely chopped fresh sage
⅓ cup (90g) honey, warmed
1 tablespoon red wine vinegar
2 cups (500ml) chicken stock
2 tablespoons cornflour
2 tablespoons water

1 Preheat oven to 240°C/220°C fan-forced.
2 Place pork rind, fat-side down, on oiled wire rack in large flameproof
baking dish; rub oil and salt into it. Roast, uncovered, about 30 minutes or
until crackling is crisp and browned; cool. Discard fat from baking dish.
3 Place pork, fat-side down, on board; sprinkle with half of the garlic and
half of the sage. Roll pork to enclose sage and garlic; secure with kitchen
string at 2cm intervals. Place pork on wire rack in same baking dish.
4 Reduce oven temperature to 200°C/180°C fan-forced; roast pork,
uncovered, 30 minutes. Cover with foil; reduce oven temperature to
180°C/160°C fan-forced. Roast 1 hour.
5 Combine honey, vinegar and remaining sage and garlic in small bowl.
Remove foil from pork, brush pork with half of the honey mixture. Roast,
uncovered, 30 minutes or until browned and cooked through, brushing
occasionally with remaining honey mixture. Remove pork from dish;
cover with foil.
6 Strain pan juices from baking dish into heatproof jug; remove fat from
pan juices (you will need ⅔ cup of pan juices). Add stock to baking dish;
stir in combined cornflour and water over heat until sauce boils and
thickens. Serve pork slices with sauce and crackling.

preparation time 20 minutes   **cooking time** 2 hours 45 minutes
serves 8
nutritional count per serving 71.1g total fat (24.0g saturated fat);
3804kJ (910 cal); 12.0g carbohydrate; 57.3g protein; 0.1g fibre

Roast pork with pears, apples and parsnips

Ask your butcher to score the rind, 1cm apart, across the pork in the same direction as you will slice, to make carving easier.

3 cloves garlic, crushed
2 tablespoons chopped fresh rosemary
2 tablespoons chopped fresh sage
¼ cup (60ml) olive oil
2kg piece boneless pork loin (not rolled)
2 tablespoons salt
2 large parsnips (360g), peeled, quartered lengthways
2 large firm pears (660g), quartered, cored
2 large red apples (400g), quartered, cored
4 cloves garlic, unpeeled, extra
¼ cup (55g) firmly packed brown sugar

1 Preheat oven to 240°C/220°C fan-forced.
2 Combine crushed garlic, rosemary, sage and 1 tablespoon of the oil; rub pork flesh (not rind) with garlic mixture. Place pork on oiled wire rack in large baking dish. Rub scored rind with salt.
3 In separate medium baking dish, combine parsnips, pears, apples, extra garlic, sugar and remaining oil.
4 Roast pork and pear mixture, uncovered, 25 minutes or until pork rind blisters. Reduce oven temperature to 180°C/160°C fan-forced; roast pork and pear mixture, uncovered, for further 45 minutes or until cooked through. Turn or shake pear mixture occasionally during cooking and remove apples when tender.
5 Remove pork and pear mixture from oven. Cover dishes with foil; stand pork for about 15 minutes before slicing.
6 Skim fat from pork pan juices; serve juices with pork and pear mixture.

preparation time 30 minutes (plus standing time)
cooking time 1 hour 10 minutes **serves** 8
nutritional count per serving 62.8g total fat (20.0g saturated fat);
3515kJ (841 cal); 22.4g carbohydrate; 46.4g protein; 3.4g fibre

263

Chinese barbecued spareribs

Ask your butcher to cut pork spareribs "american-style" for this recipe.
These will be racks of 8 to 10 ribs, cut from the mid-loin, with almost all
of the fat removed.

¾ cup (180ml) barbecue sauce
2 tablespoons dark soy sauce
1 tablespoon honey
¼ cup (60ml) orange juice
2 tablespoons brown sugar
1 clove garlic, crushed
2cm piece fresh ginger (10g), grated
2kg american-style pork spareribs

1 Combine sauces, honey, juice, sugar, garlic and ginger in large
shallow dish; add ribs, turn to coat in marinade. Cover; refrigerate
3 hours or overnight.
2 Preheat oven to 180°C/160°C fan-forced.
3 Brush ribs both sides with marinade; place, in single layer, in large
shallow baking dish; roast, covered, 45 minutes. Uncover; roast about
15 minutes or until ribs are browned. Serve with fried rice, if desired.

preparation time 15 minutes (plus refrigeration time)
cooking time 1 hour **serves** 4
nutritional count per serving 26.4g total fat (10.2g saturated fat);
2675kJ (640 cal); 35.2g carbohydrate; 64.7g protein; 0.8g fibre

Fig and ginger glazed ham

8kg cooked leg of ham
whole cloves, to decorate
2 cups (500ml) water
fig and ginger glaze
⅔ cup (230g) fig jam
½ cup (115g) glacé ginger, chopped coarsely
2 tablespoons brown sugar
¼ cup (60ml) water

1 Preheat oven to 180°C/160°C fan-forced.
2 Cut through rind 10cm from shank end of leg; run thumb around edge of rind just under skin to remove rind. Start pulling rind from shank end to widest edge of ham; discard rind. (Reserved rind can be used to cover the cut surface of ham to keep it moist during storage.)
3 Using sharp knife, score fat by making shallow cuts diagonally in both directions at 3cm intervals. Push a clove in centre of each diamond shape.
4 Make fig and ginger glaze.
5 Place ham on oiled wire rack in large baking dish; pour the water into dish. Brush ham all over with glaze. Cover shank end with foil; roast about 1 hour 20 minutes or until browned all over, brushing ham occasionally with glaze during cooking.
6 Serve ham with fresh figs, if desired.
fig and ginger glaze stir ingredients in small saucepan over low heat until sugar is dissolved. Blend or process glaze mixture until well combined.

preparation time 30 minutes **cooking time** 1 hour 20 minutes
serves 10
nutritional count per serving 45.0g total fat (15.4g saturated fat); 3929kJ (940 cal); 27.1g carbohydrate; 106.1g protein; 0.4g fibre

Pork loin with spinach and pancetta stuffing

Ask your butcher to leave a flap measuring about 20cm in length to help make rolling the stuffed loin easier.

4 slices white bread (120g)
2 tablespoons olive oil
1 clove garlic, crushed
1 medium brown onion (150g), chopped coarsely
6 slices pancetta (90g), chopped coarsely
100g baby spinach leaves
¼ cup (35g) roasted macadamias, chopped coarsely
½ cup (125ml) chicken stock
2kg boneless pork loin
plum and red wine sauce
1½ cups (480g) plum jam
2 tablespoons dry red wine
⅔ cup (160ml) chicken stock

1 Preheat oven to 200°C/180°C fan-forced.
2 Remove and discard bread crusts; cut bread into 1cm cubes. Heat half of the oil in large frying pan; cook bread, stirring, until browned and crisp. Drain croutons on absorbent paper.
3 Heat remaining oil in same pan; cook garlic, onion and pancetta until onion browns lightly. Stir in spinach; remove from heat. Gently stir in croutons, nuts and stock.
4 Place pork on board, fat-side down; slice through thickest part of pork horizontally, without cutting through other side. Open out pork to form one large piece; press stuffing mixture against loin along width of pork. Roll pork to enclose stuffing, securing with kitchen string at 2cm intervals.
5 Place rolled pork on rack in large shallow baking dish. Roast, uncovered, 1¼ hours or until cooked through.
6 Meanwhile, make plum and red wine sauce; serve with sliced pork.
plum and red wine sauce bring ingredients to the boil in small saucepan. Reduce heat; simmer, uncovered, 10 minutes or until sauce thickens slightly.
preparation time 30 minutes **cooking time** 1 hour 30 minutes
serves 10
nutritional count per serving 25.7g total fat (7.1g saturated fat); 2458kJ (588 cal); 40.3g carbohydrate; 47.0g protein; 1.8g fibre

Honey soy pork with spinach and snow pea salad

You need approximately 3 limes for this recipe.

1.6kg pork neck
4 cloves garlic, crushed
¼ cup (60ml) olive oil
2 tablespoons brown sugar
⅓ cup (115g) honey
4cm piece fresh ginger (20g), grated
¼ cup (60ml) light soy sauce
¼ cup (60ml) lime juice
spinach and snow pea salad
200g baby spinach leaves
100g snow peas, trimmed, sliced thinly
4 green onions, sliced thinly
⅓ cup (50g) roasted pine nuts, chopped coarsely
½ cup (40g) flaked parmesan cheese
⅓ cup (80ml) olive oil
1 teaspoon finely grated lime rind
¼ cup (60ml) lime juice
1 tablespoon white sugar

1 Place pork in large shallow baking dish with combined remaining ingredients. Cover; refrigerate 3 hours or overnight, turn pork occasionally.
2 Preheat oven to 180°C/160°C fan-forced.
3 Drain pork; reserve marinade. Wrap pork in three layers of foil, securing ends tightly. Roast 2 hours or until cooked through. Stand 10 minutes.
4 Meanwhile, place reserved marinade in small saucepan; bring to the boil. Reduce heat; simmer, uncovered, 5 minutes.
5 Make spinach and snow pea salad.
6 Drizzle pork with heated marinade; serve with salad.
spinach and snow pea salad place spinach, snow peas, onion, nuts and cheese in large bowl. Just before serving, add combined remaining ingredients; toss gently to combine.
preparation time 10 minutes (plus refrigeration time)
cooking time 2 hours (plus standing time) **serves** 8
nutritional count per serving 38.1g total fat (8.9g saturated fat); 2533kJ (606 cal); 18.9g carbohydrate; 46.8g protein; 1.6g fibre

Roasted pork fillets with orange

1.5kg large pork fillets
2 cloves garlic, sliced thinly lengthways
16 small fresh sage leaves
1 teaspoon fennel seeds
2 tablespoons olive oil
1 medium brown onion (150g), sliced
¾ cup (180ml) chicken stock
¼ cup (60ml) fresh orange juice

1 Cut a few small slits along the top of pork; push in garlic and sage. Sprinkle pork with seeds; stand 30 minutes.
2 Preheat oven to 220°C/200°C fan-forced.
3 Heat half of the oil in large flameproof baking dish; cook pork over heat until browned all over. Remove from dish.
4 Heat remaining oil in same dish; cook onion, stirring, until lightly browned. Return pork to dish; drizzle with stock and juice. Roast, uncovered, in oven 10 minutes or until pork is cooked through. Cover pork; stand 10 minutes.
5 Serve sliced pork with seasoned pan juices and mixed salad leaves, if desired.

preparation time 10 minutes
cooking time 35 minutes (plus standing time) **serves** 8
nutritional count per serving 19.7g total fat (5.8g saturated fat); 1446kJ (346 cal); 1.9g carbohydrate; 40.4g protein; 0.4g fibre

Honey ginger-glazed ham

8kg cooked leg of ham
2 teaspoons (approximately 4g) cloves
⅔ cup (230g) honey
½ cup (115g) glacé ginger, chopped coarsely
½ cup (100g) firmly packed brown sugar
2¼ cups (560ml) water

1 Cut through rind about 10cm from shank end of leg in decorative pattern; run thumb around edge of rind just under skin to remove rind. Start pulling rind from widest edge of ham, continue to pull carefully away from fat up to decorative pattern; discard rind. (Reserved rind can be used to cover the cut surface of ham to keep it moist during storage.)
2 Using sharp knife, score fat by making shallow cuts diagonally in both directions at 3cm intervals. Push a clove in centre of each diamond shape.
3 Preheat oven to 180°C/160°C fan-forced.
4 Stir honey, ginger, sugar and ¼ cup (60ml) of the water in small saucepan over low heat until sugar dissolves. Blend or process mixture until smooth.
5 Pour remaining water into large baking dish; place ham on oiled wire rack over dish. Brush ham all over with glaze; cover shank end with foil. Roast, uncovered, about 1 hour or until browned all over, brushing frequently with glaze during cooking.

preparation time 30 minutes **cooking time** 1 hour 5 minutes
serves 10
nutritional count per serving 33.8g total fat (12.4g saturated fat); 3733kJ (893 cal); 38.0g carbohydrate; 108.4g protein; 0.1g fibre

Pork loin with couscous and apples

1 cup (200g) couscous
1 cup (250ml) boiling water
⅓ cup (55g) seeded prunes, chopped finely
1 tablespoon roasted pine nuts
2 tablespoons coarsely chopped fresh coriander
¼ cup coarsely chopped fresh flat-leaf parsley
500g boneless pork loin, rind off
2½ cups (625ml) alcoholic apple cider
2 medium apples (300g), peeled, cored, sliced thickly
1 large red onion (300g), cut into thick wedges
2 tablespoons brown sugar

1 Preheat oven to 200°C/180°C fan-forced.
2 Combine couscous with the water in medium heatproof bowl. Cover; stand 5 minutes or until water is absorbed, fluffing with fork occasionally. Using fork, toss prunes, nuts, coriander and parsley into couscous.
3 Remove any excess fat from pork. Place pork on board, upside-down; slice through thickest part of pork horizontally, without cutting through at the other side. Open pork out to form one large piece; press 1 cup of the couscous mixture against loin along width of pork. Roll pork to enclose stuffing, securing with kitchen string at 2cm intervals.
4 Place rolled pork on oiled wire rack in large shallow flameproof baking dish; pour 2 cups of the cider over pork. Roast, uncovered, 50 minutes or until cooked through. Remove pork from dish; cover to keep warm.
5 Place remaining couscous mixture in small ovenproof dish; cook, covered, in oven about 10 minutes or until heated through.
6 Meanwhile, heat pan juices in baking dish, add remaining cider, apple, onion and sugar; cook, stirring, until apple is just tender.
7 Serve sliced pork with apple mixture and couscous.

preparation time 35 minutes **cooking time** 1 hour **serves** 4
nutritional count per serving 8.1g total fat (2.0g saturated fat); 3044kJ (727 cal); 111.1g carbohydrate; 32.3g protein; 4.6g fibre
tip to simplify the recipe, ask your butcher to remove any excess fat and butterfly the pork for you.

Pork loin with prunes, potatoes and pears

1 cup (70g) stale multigrain breadcrumbs
3 cloves garlic, crushed
1 tablespoon coarsely chopped fresh sage
¼ cup (40g) seeded prunes, chopped coarsely
¼ cup (45g) finely chopped dried figs
2 tablespoons greek-style yogurt
1.7kg lean pork loin
1 tablespoon lemon juice
1 tablespoon coarse cooking salt
2 medium brown onions (300g), cut into wedges
3 small beurre bosc pears (440g), quartered
1kg kipfler potatoes, halved lengthways
2 tablespoons olive oil

1 Preheat the oven to 240°C/220°C fan-forced.
2 Combine breadcrumbs, garlic, sage, prunes, figs and yogurt in small bowl. Place mixture against the pork loin along the length. Roll pork to enclose seasoning; secure with kitchen string at 2cm intervals.
3 Place pork on oiled wire rack in medium baking dish; rub with combined juice and salt. Roast, uncovered, about 20 minutes or until skin blisters. Drain fat from dish. Reduce oven temperature to 180°C/160°C fan-forced; add onion and pear to dish, roast, uncovered, 20 minutes.
4 Place combined potatoes and oil in separate medium baking dish; roast, uncovered, 50 minutes or until pork is cooked through and potatoes are tender.
5 Serve pork with onion, pears and potatoes.

preparation time 40 minutes **cooking time** 1 hour 10 minutes
serves 6
nutritional count per serving 70.6g total fat (22.8g saturated fat); 4452kJ (1065 cal); 46.3g carbohydrate; 58.7g protein; 8.1g fibre

Roasted char siu pork spareribs

Ask your butcher to slice spareribs thinly, about 2cm thick. Recipe can be prepared two days ahead; reheat ribs in a hot oven before serving.

1kg pork belly spareribs
¾ cup (180ml) char siu sauce
½ cup (125ml) chicken stock
1 clove garlic, crushed

1 Cut ribs into serving-sized pieces; remove rind if desired.
2 Combine rib pieces in large bowl with remaining ingredients. Cover; refrigerate 3 hours or overnight, stirring mixture occasionally.
3 Preheat oven to 200°C/180°C fan-forced.
4 Line base and sides of large baking dish with foil or pour enough boiling water into dish to just cover base. Place ribs on oiled wire rack in dish; reserve marinade. Roast, uncovered, 25 minutes or until ribs are tender and browned, brushing twice with reserved marinade during cooking.

preparation time 10 minutes (plus refrigeration time)
cooking time 25 minutes **makes** about 36 pieces
nutritional count per piece 6.5g total fat (2.2g saturated fat); 368kJ (88 cal); 2.0g carbohydrate; 5.2g protein; 0.6g fibre

Baked ham with redcurrant and balsamic glaze

¾ cup (290g) redcurrant jelly
2 tablespoons balsamic vinegar
¼ cup (50g) firmly packed brown sugar
3 cloves
8kg leg of ham
1 cup (250ml) water
20 baby onions (600g)

1 Preheat oven to 180°C/160°C fan-forced.
2 Stir jelly, vinegar, sugar and cloves in medium saucepan over medium heat until sugar is dissolved. Reserve ¼ cup glaze for the onions.
3 Cut through rind about 10cm from shank end of leg in decorative pattern; run thumb around edge of rind just under skin to remove rind. Start pulling rind from widest edge of ham, continue to pull carefully away from fat up to decorative pattern; discard rind. (Reserved rind can be used to cover the cut surface of ham to keep it moist during storage.)
4 Using sharp knife, score fat by making shallow cuts diagonally in both directions at 3cm intervals. Place ham on oiled wire rack in a large baking dish; pour in the water. Brush ham all over with glaze. Cover shank end with foil; roast, uncovered, 45 minutes.
5 Meanwhile, add onions to small baking dish with reserved ¼ cup glaze and 2 tablespoons water. Cover with foil; roast alongside ham for further 45 minutes or until tender. Brush ham with glaze every 30 minutes.
6 Serve ham with onions.

preparation time 30 minutes **cooking time** 1 hour 30 minutes
serves 10
nutritional count per serving 33.8g total fat (12.4g saturated fat); 3566kJ (853 cal); 26.8g carbohydrate; 109.1g protein; 1.1g fibre

Slow-roasted pork with fennel

1.5kg pork neck
1 clove garlic, crushed
1 teaspoon fennel seeds
1 tablespoon olive oil
⅔ cup (160ml) dry white wine
⅓ cup (80ml) chicken stock
6 medium fennel bulbs (1.8kg), halved lengthways
80g butter, softened
3 cloves garlic, sliced thinly

1 Tie pork with kitchen string at 2cm intervals. Combine crushed garlic and seeds; rub over pork.
2 Preheat oven to 150°C/130°C fan-forced.
3 Heat oil in large flameproof baking dish; cook pork, uncovered, over heat until browned all over. Add wine and stock; bring to the boil. Cover dish tightly with foil; roast, covered, in oven 1½ hours.
4 Add fennel to dish, dot with combined butter and sliced garlic; roast, covered, further 1¼ hours, turning pork and fennel occasionally.
5 Increase oven temperature to 220°C/200°C fan-forced. Remove foil from pork, spoon pan juices over pork and fennel; roast, uncovered, about 20 minutes or until browned. Transfer pork and fennel to serving platter, cover; stand 15 minutes.
6 Meanwhile, place baking dish over heat; bring pan juices to the boil. Reduce heat; simmer, uncovered, until mixture reduces to about 2 cups.
7 Serve pork and fennel drizzled with pan juices.

preparation time 25 minutes
cooking time 3 hours 25 minutes (plus standing time) **serves** 6
nutritional count per serving 34.2g total fat (14.4g saturated fat); 2412kJ (577 cal); 5.9g carbohydrate; 55.1g protein; 5.1g fibre

Crackling pork with apple and cider sauce

Ask your butcher to score the rind, 1cm apart, across the pork in the same direction as you will slice. The rind should be scored deeply, through to the fat, to ensure the fat is rendered and the crackling will be crisp. This recipe is best made close to serving.

8-rib rack of pork (2kg)
1 tablespoon coarse cooking salt
9 baby onions (225g), halved
3 trimmed celery stalks (300g), cut into 8cm lengths
⅔ cup loosely packed fresh flat-leaf parsley leaves
apple and cider sauce
10g butter
2 shallots (50g), sliced thinly
2 medium green apples (300g), peeled, cored, sliced thinly
¾ cup (180ml) dry cider
1 tablespoon white sugar
2 teaspoons lemon juice
¼ teaspoon salt

1 Preheat oven to 240°C/220°C fan-forced. Place pork in large baking dish; rub scored rind with salt. Roast pork, uncovered, 25 minutes or until rind blisters. Drain excess fat from dish.
2 Reduce oven temperature to 180°C/160°C fan-forced. Add onions and celery to baking dish with pork. Roast pork and vegetables for a further 45 minutes or until cooked through. Turn or shake vegetables occasionally during cooking.
3 Meanwhile, make apple and cider sauce.
4 Remove pork and vegetables from oven. Cover with foil; stand pork 10 minutes before slicing. Remove vegetables from dish, toss with parsley.
5 Serve pork with sauce and vegetable mixture.
apple and cider sauce heat butter in medium saucepan; cook shallots, stirring, until softened. Add apple; cook, stirring, 2 minutes. Add cider; bring to the boil. Boil, uncovered, 1 minute. Cover, simmer, 5 to 10 minutes or until apples are tender and cider has reduced slightly. Stir in sugar, juice and salt. Blend or process apple mixture until smooth.
preparation time 20 minutes **cooking time** 1 hour 30 minutes
serves 8
nutritional count per serving 36.3g total fat (12.6g saturated fat); 2011kJ (481 cal); 7.9g carbohydrate; 29.3g protein; 1.7g fibre

Blood orange marmalade glazed ham

8kg cooked leg of ham
whole cloves, to decorate
blood orange marmalade glaze
350g jar blood orange marmalade
¼ cup (55g) brown sugar
¼ cup (60ml) orange juice

1 Preheat oven to 180°C/160°C fan-forced.
2 Cut through rind about 10cm from shank end of leg; run thumb around edge of rind just under skin to remove rind. Start pulling rind from widest edge of ham, continue to pull carefully away from fat up to the cut; remove rind. (Reserved rind can be used to cover the cut surface of ham to keep it moist during storage.)
3 Using sharp knife, score fat by making shallow cuts diagonally in both directions at 3cm intervals.
4 Make blood orange marmalade glaze.
5 Line a large baking dish with overlapping sheets of baking paper. Place ham on wire rack in baking dish; brush well with glaze. Cover shank end with foil. Roast, uncovered, 40 minutes. Push a clove in centre of each diamond shape; roast further 40 minutes or until browned all over, brushing occasionally with glaze during cooking.
6 Serve ham slices warm or cold.
blood orange marmalade glaze stir ingredients in small saucepan over low heat until sugar is dissolved.

preparation time 20 minutes   **cooking time** 1 hour 30 minutes
serves 10
nutritional count per serving 38.0g total fat (14.0g saturated fat); 3963kJ (948 cal); 28.7g carbohydrate; 122.0g protein; 0.3g fibre

seafood

Asian-spiced salmon with nashi, mint and coriander salad

2 teaspoons sichuan peppercorns, crushed
2 star anise
1 tablespoon soy sauce
2 tablespoons honey
cooking-oil spray
4 salmon fillets (800g)
2 medium nashi (400g), sliced thinly
1 fresh long red chilli, sliced thinly
1 medium red onion (170g), sliced thinly
2 green onions, sliced thinly
¾ cup loosely packed fresh mint leaves
¾ cup loosely packed fresh coriander leaves
sesame soy dressing
2 tablespoons soy sauce
¼ cup (60ml) mirin
2 teaspoons caster sugar
¼ teaspoon sesame oil

1 Preheat oven to 180°C/160°C fan-forced.
2 Dry-fry spices in small frying pan until fragrant. Add sauce and honey; bring to the boil. Reduce heat; simmer, uncovered, 2 minutes.
3 Line large shallow baking dish with foil, extending foil 5cm above long sides of dish; coat with cooking-oil spray. Place fish on foil; brush both sides with spice mixture. Roast, uncovered, about 15 minutes or until cooked as desired.
4 Meanwhile, place ingredients for sesame soy dressing in screw-top jar; shake well.
5 Place nashi in large bowl with remaining ingredients and dressing; toss gently to combine. Serve with fish.

preparation time 20 minutes **cooking time** 20 minutes **serves** 4
nutritional count per serving 17.5g total fat (3.7g saturated fat); 1864kJ (446 cal); 26.7g carbohydrate; 45.5g protein; 4.0g fibre
tip if nashi are not available, substitute with crisp green apples.

Ginger and chilli baked fish

1.6kg whole white fish
cooking-oil spray
2 limes, sliced thinly
2cm piece fresh ginger (10g), sliced thinly
1 tablespoon peanut oil
1 tablespoon fish sauce
8cm piece fresh ginger (40g), grated
1 clove garlic, crushed
2 tablespoons grated palm sugar
1 fresh large red chilli, sliced
1 tablespoon fish sauce, extra
1 tablespoon lime juice

1 Preheat oven to 220°C/200°C fan-forced.

2 Make four deep slits diagonally across both sides of fish. Place large sheet of foil, with sides overlapping, in large shallow baking dish. Coat foil with cooking-oil spray; place fish on foil. Fill cavity of fish with layers of lime and sliced ginger.

3 Combine oil, fish sauce, grated ginger and garlic in small bowl; rub mixture into cuts all over surface. Bring foil up around sides of fish to catch cooking juices; do not cover top. Roast about 20 minutes or until almost cooked through.

4 Meanwhile, combine sugar, chilli, extra fish sauce and juice in small bowl; spoon over fish. Roast 5 minutes or until fish is browned and just cooked through.

preparation time 10 minutes **cooking time** 25 minutes **serves** 4
nutritional count per serving 11.1g total fat (3.2g saturated fat); 1321kJ (316 cal); 7.7g carbohydrate; 45.3g protein; 1.0g fibre
tip you may prefer to use two 800g fish; for this size, reduce cooking time to 15 minutes.

Cajun-spiced fish with roasted corn salsa

1 clove garlic, crushed
20g butter, melted
2 teaspoons sweet paprika
½ teaspoon ground cumin
1 teaspoon ground white pepper
¼ teaspoon cayenne pepper
4 x 200g firm white fish fillets
3 trimmed fresh corn cobs (750g)
1 small red onion (100g), chopped coarsely
1 medium avocado (250g), chopped coarsely
250g cherry tomatoes, halved
2 tablespoons lime juice
¼ cup coarsely chopped fresh coriander

1 Preheat oven to 220°C/200°C fan-forced.
2 Combine garlic and butter in small jug; combine spices in small bowl.
3 Place fish on oven tray, brush both sides with garlic mixture, sprinkle with combined spices. Roast, uncovered, about 15 minutes or until browned both sides and cooked as desired.
4 Meanwhile, roast corn on heated oiled grill plate (or grill or barbecue) until browned all over. When corn is just cool enough to handle, cut kernels from cobs with a small, sharp knife.
5 Combine corn kernels in medium bowl with remaining ingredients.
6 Serve fish with salsa.

preparation time 15 minutes **cooking time** 25 minutes **serves** 4
nutritional count per serving 20.2g total fat (6.4g saturated fat); 2065kJ (494 cal); 25.7g carbohydrate; 48.3g protein; 8.4g fibre
tip we used blue-eye fillets for this recipe but you can use any firm white fish fillet you prefer.

Slow-roasted salmon with green onions and peas

300g green onions
2 medium brown onions (300g)
60g butter
2 cloves garlic, sliced thinly
½ cup (125ml) vegetable stock
1kg fresh peas, shelled (or 350g shelled peas)
1 medium lemon (150g)
1kg side salmon
1 teaspoon cracked black pepper
1 teaspoon sea salt

1 Preheat oven to 120°C/100°C fan-forced.
2 Trim roots and half of the tops from green onions. Cut brown onions into wedges.
3 Heat butter in large baking dish; cook brown onion and garlic, stirring gently, until browned lightly. Add stock and peas; roast, uncovered, about 30 minutes or until onions are soft.
4 Meanwhile, remove rind from lemon with a zester (or peel rind thinly from lemon, avoiding white pith then cut rind into thin strips); squeeze 2 tablespoons juice from lemon.
5 Add onions to baking dish; place salmon on top of onion mixture. Sprinkle salmon with rind, juice, pepper and salt. Roast, uncovered, about 20 minutes or until salmon is cooked as desired.
6 Serve salmon and vegetable mixture with pan juices.

preparation time 20 minutes **cooking time** 1 hour **serves** 6
nutritional count per serving 20.6g total fat (8.1g saturated fat);
1639kJ (392 cal); 11.4g carbohydrate; 37.9g protein; 5.6g fibre

Baked fish with ginger and soy

800g whole snapper
4cm piece fresh ginger (20g), grated
1 tablespoon peanut oil
¼ cup (60ml) chinese cooking wine
¼ cup (60ml) soy sauce
½ teaspoon white sugar
3 green onions, sliced thinly

1 Preheat oven to 200°C/180°C fan-forced.
2 Cut three deep slits in each side of fish; place fish in oiled baking dish.
3 Rub ginger into fish; drizzle with combined oil, wine, sauce and sugar. Bake fish, covered, about 25 minutes or until fish is cooked through.
4 Serve fish drizzled with some of the pan juices, topped with onion.

preparation time 10 minutes **cooking time** 25 minutes **serves** 2
nutritional count per serving 11.6g total fat (2.6g saturated fat); 1120kJ (268 cal); 3.7g carbohydrate; 32.9g protein; 0.5g fibre

Vineleaf-wrapped ocean trout with braised fennel

2 medium fennel bulbs (600g), untrimmed
1 large brown onion (200g), sliced thinly
2 cloves garlic, sliced thinly
1 tablespoon olive oil
¼ cup (60ml) orange juice
½ cup (125ml) chicken stock
¼ cup (60ml) dry white wine
8 large fresh grapevine leaves
4 x 200g ocean trout fillets
1 tablespoon finely grated orange rind
180g seedless white grapes

1 Preheat oven to 180°C/160°C fan-forced.
2 Reserve enough frond tips to make ¼ cup before trimming fennel bulbs. Slice fennel thinly then combine in large shallow baking dish with onion, garlic, oil, juice, stock and wine. Bake, covered, in oven 30 minutes. Uncover, stir; bake, uncovered, further 20 minutes or until vegetables soften, stirring occasionally.
3 Meanwhile, dip vine leaves in medium saucepan of boiling water for 10 seconds; transfer immediately to medium bowl of iced water. Drain on absorbent paper. Slightly overlap two vine leaves, vein-sides up, on board; centre one fish fillet on leaves, top with a quarter of the rind and a quarter of the reserved frond tips. Fold leaves over to enclose fish. Repeat with remaining leaves, fish, rind and frond tips. Place vine-leaf parcels on oiled oven tray; bake about 15 minutes or until fish is cooked as desired.
4 Stir grapes into hot fennel mixture; stand, covered, 2 minutes before serving with fish.

preparation time 20 minutes **cooking time** 50 minutes **serves** 4
nutritional count per serving 12.5g total fat (2.5g saturated fat); 1433kJ (342 cal); 13.6g carbohydrate; 41.0g protein; 3.8g fibre
tip available from early spring, fresh grapevine leaves can be found in most specialist greengrocers. Alternatively, you can purchase cryovac-packed-in-brine leaves from Middle-Eastern food stores; rinse and dry well before using.

Pepper-roasted barramundi

You can use any small, whole, white-fleshed fish for this recipe.

4 small whole barramundi (1.2kg)
2 tablespoons sichuan peppercorns
½ teaspoon five-spice powder
½ teaspoon salt
¼ cup (60ml) lime juice
¼ cup (60ml) peanut oil
200g dried rice stick noodles
100g fresh shiitake mushrooms, sliced thinly
1kg baby buk choy, trimmed
8cm piece fresh ginger (40g), sliced thinly
⅓ cup (80ml) oyster sauce
2 teaspoons sesame oil
¼ cup (60ml) water

1 Score each fish both sides; place on large piece of oiled foil.
2 Finely crush peppercorns, add five-spice and salt. Combine spice mixture with juice and 1 tablespoon of the peanut oil in small bowl; brush mixture over each fish. Wrap foil securely around each fish; place on oven tray. Bake about 20 minutes or until fish are cooked through.
3 Meanwhile, place noodles in large heatproof bowl, cover with boiling water, stand until just tender; drain. Toss noodles with 1 tablespoon of the peanut oil.
4 Heat remaining peanut oil in wok; stir-fry mushrooms until browned. Add buk choy and ginger; stir-fry until buk choy is just wilted. Add noodles, sauce, sesame oil and the water; stir-fry until heated through. Serve with roasted fish.

preparation time 25 minutes **cooking time** 35 minutes **serves** 4
nutritional count per serving 19.2g total fat (3.5g saturated fat); 2023kJ (484 cal); 34.6g carbohydrate; 40.5g protein; 4.5g fibre

Herb and olive fish fillets on potato

750g desiree potatoes, sliced thinly
4 cloves garlic, crushed
¾ cup coarsely chopped fresh flat-leaf parsley
¼ cup (60ml) extra virgin olive oil
4 x 200g gemfish fillets
4 drained anchovy fillets, chopped finely
12 pitted black olives, halved
1 tablespoon chopped fresh basil

1 Preheat oven to 200°C/180°C fan-forced.
2 Combine potatoes, garlic, ⅔ cup of the parsley and 2 tablespoons of the oil in medium bowl.
3 Layer potatoes in baking dish; bake, uncovered, about 50 minutes or until potato is almost tender. Place fish on potato; bake further 15 minutes.
4 Meanwhile, combine anchovies, olives, remaining parsley, basil and remaining oil in small bowl.
5 Sprinkle anchovy mixture on fish; bake further 5 minutes or until fish is just cooked through. Serve with lemon wedges, if desired.

preparation time 25 minutes **cooking time** 1 hour 10 minutes
serves 4
nutritional count per serving 28.8g total fat (6.8g saturated fat); 2220kJ (531 cal); 22.3g carbohydrate; 44.3g protein; 3.6g fibre

Salmon with herb and walnut crust

1kg piece salmon fillet
1 tablespoon extra virgin olive oil
½ cup coarsely chopped fresh flat-leaf parsley
¼ cup coarsely chopped fresh dill
1 clove garlic, crushed
2 teaspoons finely grated lemon rind
¼ cup (30g) coarsely chopped roasted walnuts
2 teaspoons lemon juice
1 tablespoon extra virgin olive oil, extra

1 Preheat oven to 200°C/180°C fan-forced.
2 Place salmon in large baking dish; brush with oil. Roast 5 minutes.
3 Meanwhile, combine remaining ingredients in medium bowl.
4 Remove salmon from oven, sprinkle with three-quarters of the parsley mixture. Roast salmon further 5 minutes. The salmon will be rare in the thicker end of the fillet – you can adjust cooking time to suit your taste.
5 Transfer salmon to serving platter; sprinkle with remaining parsley mixture. Serve with lemon wedges, if desired.

preparation time 10 minutes **cooking time** 10 minutes **serves** 6
nutritional count per serving 21.4g total fat (3.7g saturated fat); 1367kJ (327 cal); 0.3g carbohydrate; 33.4g protein; 0.7g fibre
tip herb and walnut mixture can be made several hours ahead. The salmon can be cooked several hours ahead and served cold, if preferred; otherwise, roast close to serving.

Whole fish in a salt crust with gremolata

2 x 1kg whole snapper, cleaned, scales left on
3kg coarse cooking salt, approximately
gremolata
½ cup finely chopped fresh flat-leaf parsley
2 cloves garlic, crushed
1 tablespoon finely grated lemon rind
2 tablespoons extra virgin olive oil

1 Preheat oven to 240°C/220°C fan-forced.
2 Make gremolata.
3 Wash fish, pat dry inside and out; fill cavities with half of the gremolata.
4 Divide half the salt between two ovenproof trays large enough to hold fish (ovenproof metal oval platters are ideal). Place fish on salt.
5 Place remaining salt in large sieve or colander and run quickly under cold water until salt is damp. Press salt firmly over fish to completely cover fish. Bake 35 minutes. Remove fish from oven; stand 5 minutes.
6 Using a hammer or meat mallet and old knife, break open the crust then lift away with the scales and skin. Serve fish with remaining gremolata.
gremolata combine ingredients in small bowl.

preparation time 10 minutes **cooking time** 35 minutes **serves** 8
nutritional count per serving 6.1g total fat (1.2g saturated fat);
560kJ (134 cal); 0.1g carbohydrate; 19.4g protein; 0.4g fibre
tips you can use different types of whole fish that weigh about 1kg each. Make sure the fish and tray will fit into the oven. Coarse sea salt can also be used; it is available from supermarkets or health food stores. Rock salt should not be used in this recipe.

Red snapper parcels with caper anchovy salsa

2 cloves garlic, crushed
1 baby fennel bulb (130g), sliced thinly
4 x 200g red snapper fillets
4 large fresh basil leaves
⅓ cup (80ml) dry white wine
¼ cup coarsely chopped fresh chives
⅓ cup loosely packed fresh tarragon leaves
⅓ cup loosely packed fresh basil leaves
½ cup loosely packed fresh chervil leaves
30g watercress, trimmed
1 tablespoon lemon juice
1 teaspoon olive oil
caper anchovy salsa
1 small red capsicum (150g), chopped finely
2 tablespoons finely chopped kalamata olives
1 tablespoon drained baby capers, rinsed
8 drained anchovy fillets, chopped finely
¼ cup finely chopped fresh basil
1 tablespoon balsamic vinegar

1 Preheat oven to 220°C/200°C fan-forced.
2 Combine garlic and fennel in small bowl.
3 Place fish, skin-side down, on four separate squares of oiled foil large enough to completely enclose fish. Top each fillet with equal amounts of the fennel mixture and one basil leaf; drizzle each with 1 tablespoon of the wine. Gather corners of foil squares together above each fish; twist to enclose securely.
4 Place parcels on oven tray; bake about 15 minutes or until fish is cooked as desired.
5 Meanwhile, combine ingredients for caper anchovy salsa in small bowl.
6 Place herbs and watercress in medium bowl with combined juice and oil; toss gently to combine.
7 Unwrap parcels just before serving; divide fish, fennel-side up, among serving plates. Top with salsa; accompany with salad.
preparation time 30 minutes **cooking time** 15 minutes **serves** 4
nutritional count per serving 5.3g total fat (1.5g saturated fat); 1068kJ (255 cal); 3.6g carbohydrate; 43.9 protein; 2.0g fibre

Snapper, fennel and semi-dried tomato parcels

20g butter
3 baby fennel bulbs (390g), trimmed, sliced thinly
¼ cup (60ml) water
⅔ cup (100g) semi-dried tomatoes
2 tablespoons fresh oregano leaves
3 cloves garlic, crushed
2 teaspoons finely grated lemon rind
2 tablespoons lemon juice
1 tablespoon olive oil
6 x 400g whole snapper, cleaned
herb butter
60g butter, softened
2 tablespoons finely chopped fresh oregano
2 tablespoons finely chopped fresh flat-leaf parsley

1 Preheat oven to 220°C/200°C fan-forced.
2 Make herb butter.
3 Melt butter in medium frying pan; cook fennel, stirring, until softened. Remove from heat; blend or process with the water, tomatoes, oregano, garlic, rind, juice and oil until mixture forms a paste.
4 Score each fish three times on both sides; place each fish on a square of oiled foil large enough to completely enclose fish. Top each fish with equal amounts of the fennel mixture; gather corners of foil squares together above fish, twist to enclose securely.
5 Place parcels on oven tray; bake 15 minutes or until cooked as desired.
6 Discard foil just before serving; top fish with a slice of herb butter.
herb butter beat ingredients in small bowl until combined. Place on piece of plastic wrap; shape into a log, wrap butter mixture tightly in plastic wrap. Refrigerate until firm; remove 15 minutes before serving.

preparation time 35 minutes (plus refrigeration time)
cooking time 20 minutes **serves** 6
nutritional count per serving 17.3g total fat (8.7g saturated fat); 1363kJ (326 cal); 7.5g carbohydrate; 33.3g protein; 3.9g fibre

Salt-crusted barramundi on baby buk choy with red curry sauce

4 x 300g whole baby barramundi
3 cloves garlic, sliced thinly
1 tablespoon garlic salt
2 tablespoons sea salt
2 tablespoons peanut oil
4 green onions
10cm piece fresh ginger (50g)
¼ cup finely shredded fresh coriander
¼ cup (70g) red curry paste
¾ cup (180ml) vegetable stock
½ cup (125ml) water
1 cup (250ml) coconut milk
2 fresh kaffir lime leaves, torn
500g baby buk choy, trimmed, halved

1 Preheat oven to 220°C/200°C fan-forced.
2 Score fish three times both sides; place on oiled wire rack over large baking dish. Press garlic into cuts, sprinkle with combined salts, drizzle with half of the oil. Bake, uncovered, about 30 minutes or until skin is crisp and fish is cooked as desired.
3 Meanwhile, slice onions and ginger into 5cm-long thin strips. Toss in small bowl with coriander; reserve.
4 Heat remaining oil in wok; stir-fry paste about 2 minutes or until fragrant. Add stock, the water, coconut milk and lime leaves, bring to the boil; simmer, uncovered, 5 minutes. Add buk choy; stir-fry until just wilted.
5 Serve fish with buk choy and red curry sauce; sprinkle with reserved coriander mixture.

preparation time 25 minutes **cooking time** 40 minutes **serves** 4
nutritional count per serving 30.0g total fat (14.3g saturated fat);
1910kJ (457 cal); 6.6g carbohydrate; 38.1g protein; 5.5g fibre

Tandoori salmon with pilaf and raita

4 x 200g salmon fillets
¼ cup (70g) tandoori curry paste
2 tablespoons yogurt
2 teaspoons lemon juice
2 tablespoons peanut oil
1 large white onion (200g), sliced
2 cloves garlic, sliced
½ teaspoon cumin seeds
½ teaspoon coriander seeds
⅛ teaspoon ground turmeric
1½ cups (300g) basmati rice
3½ cups (875ml) chicken stock
2 teaspoons grated lemon rind
cucumber and mint raita
½ medium lebanese cucumber (75g)
1 tablespoon chopped fresh mint
¾ cup (200g) yogurt

1 Place salmon in non-metallic dish; pour combined paste, yogurt and juice over fish. (If time permits, cover and refrigerate 2 hours.)
2 Meanwhile, preheat oven to 200°C/180°C fan-forced.
3 Heat oil in flameproof baking dish; cook onion, garlic and spices, stirring over heat, until onion softens. Add rice; stir until coated with oil. Stir in stock and rind; bring to the boil. Remove from heat, cover tightly with lid or foil; roast in oven 15 minutes.
4 Uncover rice, top with salmon; roast further 8 minutes or until salmon is cooked as desired.
5 Meanwhile, make cucumber and mint raita.
6 Serve salmon with rice and raita; sprinkle with coriander, if desired.
cucumber and mint raita halve cucumber lengthways; remove and discard seeds. Chop cucumber finely; combine with mint and yogurt in small bowl.

preparation time 20 minutes (plus refrigeration time)
cooking time 35 minutes **serves** 4
nutritional count per serving 32.2g total fat (7.3g saturated fat); 3244kJ (776 cal); 68.4g carbohydrate; 51.1g protein; 3.6g fibre

Slow-roasted salmon with asian greens

750g piece salmon fillet, boned, with skin on
1 fresh kaffir lime, quartered
1 tablespoon finely shredded fresh kaffir lime leaves
½ cup (110g) caster sugar
¼ cup (60ml) lime juice
¼ cup (60ml) water
2 fresh small red thai chillies, chopped finely
¼ cup finely chopped fresh coriander leaves
1 tablespoon peanut oil
250g asparagus, trimmed, chopped coarsely
150g snow peas
150g baby buk choy, chopped coarsely
150g choy sum, chopped coarsely

1 Preheat oven to 120°C/100°C fan-forced.
2 Cook fish and quartered lime on heated oiled grill plate (or grill or barbecue) until both are lightly coloured all over.
3 Place fish and lime in oiled large baking dish; sprinkle with lime leaves. Bake, covered tightly, in oven 30 minutes or until cooked as desired.
4 Meanwhile, stir sugar, juice and the water in small saucepan over heat, without boiling, until sugar dissolves. Simmer, uncovered, without stirring, 3 minutes; cool slightly. Stir in chilli and coriander.
5 Heat oil in wok; stir-fry asparagus and snow peas until just tender. Add buk choy and choy sum with half of the chilli sauce; stir-fry until leaves are just wilted.
6 Serve vegetables with fish, drizzled with remaining chilli sauce.

preparation time 15 minutes **cooking time** 40 minutes **serves** 4
nutritional count per serving 18.2g total fat (3.8g saturated fat); 1910kJ (457 cal); 31.2g carbohydrate; 40.3g protein; 2.9g fibre

Fish in prosciutto with capers and garlic mayonnaise

For this recipe, be sure the prosciutto is very thinly sliced.

6 x 360g plate-sized white fish (barramundi, bream, snapper)
2 tablespoons finely grated lemon rind
5 cloves garlic, sliced thinly
1½ cups coarsely chopped fresh flat-leaf parsley leaves
18 slices thin prosciutto (220g)
1 tablespoon drained capers, chopped
garlic mayonnaise
½ cup (150g) mayonnaise
1 tablespoon lemon juice
1 clove garlic, crushed

1 Preheat the oven to 220°C/200°C fan-forced. Line oven trays with baking paper.
2 Wash cavity of fish under cold water; pat dry with absorbent paper.
3 Combine rind, garlic, and parsley in medium bowl; fill fish cavities with parsley mixture. Wrap three slices of the prosciutto around each fish.
4 Place fish on trays; bake 15 minutes. Sprinkle capers over fish; bake further 5 minutes or until fish is just cooked through.
5 Meanwhile, make garlic mayonnaise.
6 Serve fish with mayonnaise and lemon wedges, if desired.
garlic mayonnaise combine ingredients in small bowl.

preparation time 15 minutes **cooking time** 20 minutes **serves** 6
nutritional count per serving 14.5g total fat (3.1g saturated fat);
1430kJ (342 cal); 5.7g carbohydrate; 46.3g protein; 1.6g fibre

Slow-roasted pesto salmon

1 cup loosely packed fresh basil leaves
2 cloves garlic, chopped coarsely
2 tablespoons roasted pine nuts
2 tablespoons lemon juice
¼ cup (60ml) olive oil
1.5kg piece salmon fillet, skin on
2 tablespoons olive oil, extra
2 large red capsicums (700g), chopped coarsely
1 large red onion (300g), chopped coarsely

1 Preheat oven to 160°C/140°C fan-forced.
2 Blend or process basil, garlic, nuts and juice until combined. With motor operating, gradually add oil in thin, steady stream until pesto thickens slightly.
3 Place fish, skin-side down, on piece of oiled foil large enough to completely enclose fish; coat fish with half of the pesto. Gather corners of foil together above fish; twist to enclose securely. Place parcel on oven tray; roast about 45 minutes or until cooked as desired.
4 Meanwhile, heat extra oil in large frying pan; cook capsicum and onion, stirring, until onion softens.
5 Serve salmon topped with onion mixture, drizzled with remaining pesto.

preparation time 20 minutes **cooking time** 45 minutes **serves** 8
nutritional count per serving 27.5g total fat (4.8g saturated fat); 1802kJ (431 cal); 6.1g carbohydrate; 39.2g protein; 2.0g fibre
tip if the pesto is a little too thick for your liking, thin it down with a little olive oil before drizzling over the salmon.

Slow-roasted ocean trout and asian greens

8 x 100g ocean trout fillets
2 fresh kaffir lime leaves, shredded finely
10cm stick fresh lemon grass (20g), chopped finely
1 teaspoon sesame oil
250g baby buk choy, quartered
250g choy sum, chopped coarsely
2 teaspoons light soy sauce
⅓ cup (80ml) sweet chilli sauce
¼ cup (60ml) lime juice

1 Preheat oven to 150°C/130°C fan-forced.
2 Place four fish fillets, skin-side down, on board; sprinkle with lime leaves and lemon grass. Top with remaining fish fillets, skin-side up; tie together with kitchen string.
3 Place fish in large shallow baking dish; roast, uncovered, 15 minutes.
4 Meanwhile, heat oil in wok; stir-fry buk choy, choy sum and soy sauce until vegetables just wilt.
5 Serve fish with stir-fried vegetables; drizzle with combined chilli sauce and juice.

preparation time 15 minutes **cooking time** 20 minutes **serves** 4
nutritional count per serving 9.6g total fat (2.1g saturated fat); 1158kJ (277 cal); 5.3g carbohydrate; 40.6g protein; 2.5g fibre

Barramundi with kipflers and roasted capsicum

We used a whole barramundi for this recipe, but any whole, firm, white-fleshed large fish can be used.

700g kipfler potatoes, halved lengthways
½ cup (125ml) vegetable stock
1 tablespoon lemon juice
1 tablespoon finely grated lemon rind
⅓ cup coarsely chopped fresh oregano
1.2kg whole barramundi, cleaned
1 large red capsicum (350g), sliced thinly
1 large yellow capsicum (350g), sliced thinly
2 cloves garlic, crushed

1 Preheat oven to 180°C/160°C fan-forced.
2 Combine potato, stock and juice in large baking dish; roast, uncovered, 10 minutes.
3 Meanwhile, combine rind and oregano in small bowl. Score fish both sides; press rind mixture into cuts and inside cavity.
4 Place fish in oiled large baking dish; roast, uncovered, 30 minutes.
5 Meanwhile, add capsicums and garlic to potato mixture; stir to combine. Roast, uncovered, further 30 minutes or until potato is tender.
6 Serve fish with vegetables, drizzled with any pan juices; sprinkle fish with oregano leaves, if desired.

preparation time 25 minutes **cooking time** 40 minutes **serves** 4
nutritional count per serving 2.5g total fat (0.7g saturated fat);
1296kJ (310 cal); 28.1g carbohydrate; 40.5g protein; 5.3g fibre

Salt-baked whole ocean trout in saffron cream sauce

3kg cooking salt
4 egg whites
2.4kg whole ocean trout
1.5kg baby new potatoes
3 whole unpeeled bulbs garlic, halved horizontally
¼ cup (60ml) olive oil
15 sprigs fresh thyme
350g watercress, trimmed
saffron cream sauce
¾ cup (180ml) dry white wine
¼ cup (60ml) white wine vinegar
1 tablespoon lemon juice
pinch saffron threads
½ cup (125ml) cream
170g butter, chilled, chopped finely

1 Preheat oven to 200°C/180°C fan-forced.
2 Mix salt with egg whites in medium bowl. Spread about half of the salt mixture evenly over base of large baking dish; place fish on salt mixture, cover completely (except for tail) with remaining salt mixture. Bake 1 hour.
3 Meanwhile, combine potatoes, garlic, oil and thyme in large shallow baking dish; place in oven on shelf below fish. Bake, uncovered, about 50 minutes or until potatoes are tender.
4 Make saffron cream sauce.
5 Remove fish from oven; break salt crust with heavy knife, taking care not to cut into fish. Discard salt crust; transfer fish to large serving plate. Carefully remove skin from fish; flake meat into large pieces.
6 Divide watercress, potatoes and garlic among serving plates; top with fish, drizzle with sauce.
saffron cream sauce bring wine, vinegar, juice and saffron in medium saucepan to the boil. Boil until mixture is reduced to about a third. Add cream; return to the boil, then whisk in butter, one piece at a time, until mixture thickens slightly. Pour into medium jug; cover to keep warm.
preparation time 30 minutes **cooking time** 1 hour 10 minutes
serves 6
nutritional count per serving 50.4g total fat (24.6g saturated fat); 3528kJ (844 cal); 36.2g carbohydrate; 52.4g protein; 9.8g fibre

Crisp-skinned thai chilli snapper

1.2 kg whole snapper
4 cloves garlic, crushed
2 x 10cm sticks fresh lemon grass (40g), chopped finely
¼ cup chopped fresh coriander
2 fresh small red thai chillies, chopped finely
2 tablespoons sweet chilli sauce
4cm piece fresh ginger (20g), grated
1 tablespoon thai red curry paste
2 tablespoons lime juice
2 tablespoons sweet chilli sauce, extra
½ cup firmly packed fresh coriander leaves, extra

1 Make four deep slits diagonally across both sides of fish; place fish in shallow non-metallic baking dish.
2 Pour combined remaining ingredients, except extra chilli sauce and extra coriander leaves, over fish. Cover; refrigerate 3 hours or overnight.
3 Preheat oven to 180ºC/160ºC fan-forced.
4 Cover dish with foil; bake 35 minutes or until fish is almost tender.
5 Brush fish with extra chilli sauce then grill about 10 minutes or until skin is browned and crisp. Serve topped with extra coriander leaves.

preparation time 15 minutes (plus refrigeration time)
cooking time 45 minutes **serves** 6
nutritional count per serving 2.9g total fat (0.7g saturated fat); 451kJ (108 cal); 3.5g carbohydrate; 16.1g protein; 1.6g fibre

Roast salmon with mango and lime mayonnaise

3kg whole salmon
1 medium lime, sliced thinly
3 sprigs fresh dill
cooking-oil spray
¼ cup (60ml) olive oil
2 tablespoons drained capers
mango and lime mayonnaise
2 egg yolks
½ teaspoon dry mustard
½ cup (125ml) light olive oil
¼ cup (60ml) olive oil
2 tablespoons lime juice
1 teaspoon finely grated lime rind
1 medium mango (430g), peeled, quartered

1 Preheat oven to 180°C/200°C fan-forced.
2 Wash fish, pat dry inside and out with absorbent paper; place lime and dill inside cavity. Place two large pieces of foil, overlapping slightly, on oven tray; coat with cooking oil-spray. Place fish on foil, fold foil over to completely enclose fish. Roast about 1 hour or until cooked as desired.
3 Meanwhile, heat oil in small frying pan; cook capers, stirring, until crisp. Drain on absorbent paper.
4 Make mango and lime mayonnaise.
5 Starting behind gills of salmon, peel away and discard skin; scrape away any dark flesh. Flake salmon coarsely; sprinkle with capers.
6 Serve salmon warm or cold with mayonnaise.
mango and lime mayonnaise blend or process egg yolks and mustard until smooth. With motor operating, add combined oils gradually in thin stream until mixture is thick. Add remaining ingredients; blend until smooth.

preparation time 30 minutes **cooking time** 1 hour 10 minutes
serves 8
nutritional count per serving 43.7g total fat (7.6g saturated fat); 2391kJ (572 cal); 5.3g carbohydrate; 40.0g protein; 0.8g fibre
tip salmon is best served rare in the centre so it remains moist.

vegetables

Maple-glazed sweet potato and red onions

4 medium white sweet potatoes (1.6kg)
2 tablespoons lemon juice
4 medium red onions (680g), quartered
2 tablespoons extra virgin olive oil
2 tablespoons maple syrup
sea salt flakes

1 Preheat oven to 180°C/160°C fan-forced. Line shallow oven tray with baking paper.
2 Peel sweet potatoes; place in bowl of cold water with juice to prevent browning. Cut potatoes into thick slices, return to lemon water.
3 Drain potato, pat dry with absorbent paper. Place potato and onion on tray. Drizzle vegetables with oil; drizzle sweet potato only with maple syrup. Sprinkle with salt.
4 Roast vegetables about 40 minutes or until tender and browned.

preparation time 15 minutes **cooking time** 40 minutes **serves** 8
nutritional count per serving 4.8g total fat (0.6g saturated fat);
932kJ (223 cal); 38.6g carbohydrate; 3.6g protein; 4.5g fibre

Stuffed capsicums with lentils

1 tablespoon olive oil
1 small brown onion (80g), chopped finely
1 clove garlic, crushed
1 small carrot (70g), chopped finely
1 small green zucchini (90g), chopped finely
¼ cup (60ml) water
¼ cup (50g) red lentils
¼ cup (55g) risoni
1 tablespoon tomato paste
1 cup (250ml) vegetable stock
12 baby red capsicums (540g)
2 tablespoons finely grated parmesan cheese

1 Preheat oven to 220°C/200°C fan-forced. Line oven tray with baking paper.
2 Heat oil in large saucepan; cook onion and garlic, stirring, until onion softens. Add carrot and zucchini; cook, stirring, until vegetables are tender. Stir in the water, lentils, risoni, paste and stock; bring to the boil. Reduce heat; simmer, uncovered, 10 minutes or until lentils are tender.
3 Meanwhile, carefully cut tops off capsicums; discard tops. Discard seeds and membranes, leaving capsicums intact. Place on tray; roast, uncovered, about 15 minutes or until just softened.
4 Divide lentil mixture among capsicums; sprinkle with cheese. Place under preheated grill until cheese melts.

preparation time 15 minutes **cooking time** 30 minutes **serves** 4
nutritional count per serving 6.7g total fat (1.5g saturated fat); 815kJ (195 cal); 22.0g carbohydrate; 9.3g protein; 4.9g fibre

Roast potato, onion and red capsicum salad

1kg new potatoes, halved
1 medium red onion (170g), cut into thin wedges
1 large red capsicum (350g), chopped coarsely
2 teaspoons olive oil
80g baby rocket leaves
300g can red kidney beans, rinsed, drained
100g low-fat fetta, diced into 1cm pieces
2 tablespoons coarsely chopped fresh flat-leaf parsley
honey balsamic dressing
1 tablespoon honey
2 teaspoons balsamic vinegar
2 teaspoons water
2 teaspoons olive oil

1 Preheat oven to 220°C/200°C fan-forced.
2 Combine potato, onion, capsicum and oil in large deep baking dish; roast, uncovered, about 40 minutes or until vegetables are browned and tender, stirring halfway through cooking time.
3 Place ingredients for honey balsamic dressing in screw-top jar; shake well.
4 Place roasted vegetables in large bowl with rocket, beans, cheese, parsley and dressing; toss gently to combine.

preparation time 15 minutes **cooking time** 40 minutes **serves** 4
nutritional count per serving 9.1g total fat (3.0g saturated fat); 1501kJ (359 cal); 50.5g carbohydrate; 17.9g protein; 9.4g fibre

Roasted root vegetables

1 tablespoon olive oil
10 baby carrots (200g), peeled, halved lengthways
2 small parsnips (120g), peeled, quartered lengthways
8 baby potatoes (320g), halved
3 baby onions (75g), halved
1 clove garlic, crushed
1 tablespoon fresh rosemary
1 tablespoon honey
2 teaspoons wholegrain mustard
1 tablespoon lemon juice

1 Preheat oven to 220°C/200°C fan-forced.
2 Heat oil in flameproof baking dish; cook carrot, parsnip, potato and onion over heat until lightly browned, turning occasionally. Remove from heat; stir in garlic, rosemary, honey and mustard.
3 Roast vegetables, uncovered, in oven about 20 minutes or until vegetables are tender.
4 Serve vegetables drizzled with juice.

preparation time 10 minutes **cooking time** 30 minutes **serves** 2
nutritional count per serving 9.7g total fat (1.3g saturated fat); 1279kJ (306 cal); 44.3g carbohydrate; 6.3g protein; 7.8g fibre

Middle-eastern roasted pumpkin, carrot and parsnip

900g piece pumpkin, unpeeled, sliced thinly
1 tablespoon olive oil
4 large carrots (720g), halved, sliced thickly
2 large parsnips (700g), chopped coarsely
⅓ cup firmly packed fresh flat-leaf parsley leaves
¼ cup (40g) roasted pine nuts
spice paste
2 cloves garlic, quartered
1 teaspoon cumin seeds
1 teaspoon coriander seeds
½ teaspoon ground cinnamon
1 teaspoon sea salt
1 tablespoon olive oil
20g butter
¼ cup (55g) firmly packed brown sugar
1½ cups (375ml) apple juice

1 Preheat oven to 200°C/180°C fan-forced.
2 Combine pumpkin and oil in large baking dish. Roast, uncovered, about 25 minutes or until just tender.
3 Meanwhile, boil, steam or microwave carrot and parsnip, separately, until just tender; drain.
4 Make spice paste.
5 Place vegetables, parsley and nuts in large bowl with spice mixture; toss gently to combine.
spice paste using mortar and pestle or small electric spice blender, crush garlic, cumin, coriander, cinnamon, salt and oil until mixture forms a thick paste. Melt butter in large frying pan; cook paste, stirring, about 3 minutes or until fragrant. Add sugar and juice; bring to the boil. Cook, stirring, about 10 minutes or until spice mixture thickens slightly.

preparation time 20 minutes **cooking time** 25 minutes **serves** 8
nutritional count per serving 10.7g total fat (2.5g saturated fat); 1032kJ (247 cal); 29.9g carbohydrate; 4.8g protein; 5.8g fibre

Roast potatoes

6 pontiac potatoes (1.3kg), peeled, halved horizontally
2 tablespoons light olive oil

1 Preheat oven to 220°C/200°C fan-forced. Oil oven tray.
2 Boil, steam or microwave potatoes 5 minutes; drain. Pat dry with absorbent paper; cool 10 minutes.
3 Gently rake rounded sides of potatoes with tines of fork; place in single layer, cut-side down, on tray. Brush potatoes with oil.
4 Roast potatoes, uncovered, 50 minutes or until browned and crisp.

preparation time 10 minutes (plus cooling time)
cooking time 55 minutes **serves** 4
nutritional count per serving 9.4g total fat (1.3g saturated fat); 1062kJ (254 cal); 34.1g carbohydrate; 6.2g protein; 4.2g fibre
tips olive oil is better to brush potatoes with than any other oil or butter as it tolerates high oven temperatures and lends its pleasant taste to the potatoes. Gently raking along the length of the peeled potato surface with the tines of a fork assists in crisping. Don't crowd potatoes on the oven tray because they will brown unevenly, and ensure the oven has reached the correct temperature before the tray goes in. Kipfler, lasoda and pink-eye potatoes are also good for roasting.

Roasted beetroot and onion

2 tablespoons olive oil
10 medium unpeeled fresh beetroot (1.6kg), halved
20 baby onions (500g), peeled
2 tablespoons red wine vinegar
2 tablespoons olive oil, extra
2 tablespoons coarsely chopped fresh flat-leaf parsley

1 Preheat oven to 240°C/220°C fan-forced.
2 Brush base of baking dish with half of the oil, add beetroot; cover tightly with foil. Roast 45 minutes.
3 Combine onions with remaining oil, add to beetroot; cover tightly with foil. Roast 30 minutes or until vegetables are tender. Remove foil; roast further 10 minutes.
4 Wearing rubber gloves, remove skin from hot beetroot; cut beetroot in half. Place beetroot and onion in serving dish; drizzle with combined vinegar and extra oil, sprinkle with parsley and freshly ground black pepper.

preparation time 25 minutes **cooking time** 1 hour 25 minutes
serves 6
nutritional count per serving 12.5g total fat (1.7g saturated fat);
991kJ (237 cal); 21.9g carbohydrate; 5.5g protein; 8.0g fibre

Oven-roasted ratatouille with couscous

1 medium eggplant (300g), chopped coarsely
6 small tomatoes (540g), peeled, chopped coarsely
4 cloves garlic, sliced thinly
1 tablespoon olive oil
2 tablespoons tomato paste
1 large red onion (300g), chopped coarsely
1 small red capsicum (150g), chopped coarsely
1 small green capsicum (150g), chopped coarsely
2 medium zucchini (240g), chopped coarsely
1½ cups (375ml) vegetable stock
1½ cups (300g) couscous
½ cup finely chopped fresh flat-leaf parsley

1 Preheat oven to 200°C/180°C fan-forced.
2 Combine eggplant, tomato, garlic, oil, paste, onion, capsicum and zucchini in large baking dish. Roast, covered, 40 minutes. Uncover; roast about 20 minutes or until vegetables are tender.
3 Meanwhile, bring stock to the boil in large saucepan. Stir in couscous; cover, stand about 5 minutes or until stock is absorbed, fluffing with fork occasionally. Stir in parsley.
4 Serve ratatouille with couscous.

preparation time 30 minutes **cooking time** 1 hour **serves** 4
nutritional count per serving 6.2g total fat (0.9g saturated fat);
1714kJ (410 cal); 71.1g carbohydrate; 16.2g protein; 7.9g fibre

Hasselback potatoes

6 desiree potatoes (1.1kg), peeled, halved horizontally
40g butter, melted
2 tablespoons olive oil
¼ cup (25g) packaged breadcrumbs
½ cup (60g) finely grated cheddar cheese

1 Preheat oven to 180°C/160°C fan-forced.
2 Place one potato half, cut-side down, on chopping board; place a chopstick on board along each side of potato. Slice potato thinly, cutting down to chopsticks to prevent cutting all the way through. Repeat with remaining potato halves.
3 Coat potato halves in combined butter and oil in medium baking dish; place, rounded-side up, in single layer. Roast, uncovered, 45 minutes, brushing frequently with oil mixture. Continue roasting without brushing about 15 minutes or until potatoes are cooked through.
4 Sprinkle combined breadcrumbs and cheese over potatoes; roast, uncovered, about 10 minutes or until topping is browned lightly.

preparation time 20 minutes **cooking time** 1 hour 10 minutes
serves 4
nutritional count per serving 22.8g total fat (10.0g saturated fat); 1605kJ (384 cal); 33.0g carbohydrate; 10.0g protein; 3.8g fibre

Roasted vegetable and balsamic salad

¼ cup (60ml) olive oil
1 clove garlic, crushed
2 large green zucchini (300g)
4 medium flat mushrooms (500g), quartered
4 large egg tomatoes (360g), quartered
1 medium red onion (170g), cut into wedges
150g lamb's lettuce, trimmed
⅓ cup coarsely chopped fresh basil
dressing
¼ cup (60ml) olive oil
2 tablespoons balsamic vinegar
½ teaspoon white sugar
½ teaspoon dijon mustard
1 clove garlic, crushed

1 Preheat oven to 220°C/200°C fan-forced.
2 Combine oil and garlic in small bowl.
3 Halve zucchini lengthways then chop into thin wedge-shaped pieces on the diagonal.
4 Arrange all vegetable pieces, in single layer, on oven trays, brush with garlic-flavoured oil; roast, uncovered, about 20 minutes or until browned lightly and just tender. Remove vegetables from oven; cool.
5 Place ingredients for dressing in screw-top jar; shake well.
6 Place cold vegetables in large bowl with lettuce, basil and dressing; toss gently to combine.

preparation time 10 minutes **cooking time** 25 minutes **serves** 4
nutritional count per serving 28.1g total fat (3.9g saturated fat); 1329kJ (318 cal); 6.5g carbohydrate; 7.4g protein; 7.0g fibre
tips combine garlic and oil a day ahead, and cover at room temperature, in order to infuse the oil with the full flavour of the garlic.
Lamb's lettuce, also known as mâche, lamb's tongue or corn salad, has clusters of tiny, tender, nutty-tasting leaves; mild and succulent, lamb's lettuce does not overpower any ingredient it accompanies, but instead allows the other flavours to dominate. You can substitute mesclun, baby mixed salad leaves or butter lettuce, if lamb's lettuce is not available.

Roast pumpkin and potato with garlic and rosemary

750g butternut pumpkin, chopped coarsely
750g medium potatoes, chopped coarsely
1 tablespoon olive oil
2 cloves garlic, sliced thinly
2 tablespoons fresh rosemary
2 teaspoons sea salt

1 Preheat oven to 220°C/200°C fan-forced.
2 Combine pumpkin, potato, oil and garlic in large baking dish. Roast, uncovered, about 1 hour or until vegetables are just tender and browned lightly. Sprinkle with rosemary and salt.

preparation time 15 minutes **cooking time** 1 hour **serves** 4
nutritional count per serving 5.7g total fat (1.1g saturated fat); 882kJ (211 cal); 30.4g carbohydrate; 6.9g protein; 4.7g fibre

Roasted baby carrots with garlic

3 bunches baby carrots (1kg)
¼ cup (60ml) olive oil
2 cloves garlic, crushed
2 teaspoons honey
1 tablespoon fresh thyme leaves

1 Preheat oven to 220°C/200°C fan-forced.
2 Trim carrot tops, leaving 2cm of the stems intact. Wash carrots well.
3 Place carrots in medium baking dish with combined oil, garlic and honey; toss well. Roast, uncovered, 15 minutes.
4 Add thyme leaves, roast further 3 minutes or until tender.

preparation time 15 minutes **cooking time** 20 minutes **serves** 10
nutritional count per serving 5.6g total fat (0.8g saturated fat);
343kJ (82 cal); 6.0g carbohydrate; 0.7g protein; 3.0g fibre

Capsicums stuffed with pilaf

2 teaspoons olive oil
1 medium red onion (170g), chopped finely
1 tablespoon slivered almonds
⅔ cup (130g) white long-grain rice
1 cup (250ml) water
2 tablespoons finely chopped dried apricots
¼ cup (35g) sun-dried tomatoes, chopped finely
¼ cup finely chopped fresh flat-leaf parsley
4 medium red capsicums (800g)
cooking-oil spray
roasted tomato salad
2 medium tomatoes (300g), cut into thick wedges
1 tablespoon apple cider vinegar
½ teaspoon cracked black pepper
1 teaspoon white sugar
1 cup firmly packed fresh flat-leaf parsley leaves
½ cup firmly packed fresh mint leaves

1 Preheat oven to 200°C/180°C fan-forced.
2 Heat oil in medium saucepan; cook onion and nuts, stirring, until onion softens. Add rice; cook, stirring, 1 minute. Add the water; bring to the boil. Reduce heat; simmer, covered, about 15 minutes or until liquid is absorbed and rice is just tender. Stir in apricot, tomato and parsley.
3 Carefully cut tops off capsicums; discard tops. Discard seeds and membranes, leaving capsicum intact. Divide pilaf among capsicums; place capsicums on oven tray, coat with cooking oil-spray. Roast, uncovered, 10 minutes. Cover loosely with foil; cook about 20 minutes or until capsicums are just soft.
4 Meanwhile, make roasted tomato salad. Serve with capsicums.
roasted tomato salad combine tomato with vinegar, pepper and sugar in medium bowl. Drain; reserve liquid. Place tomato on oven tray; roast, uncovered, alongside capsicums about 10 minutes or until tomato just softens. Place tomato and reserved liquid in medium bowl with herbs; toss gently to combine.

preparation time 20 minutes **cooking time** 55 minutes **serves** 4
nutritional count per serving 5.7g total fat (0.6g saturated fat);
1087kJ (260 cal); 43.4g carbohydrate; 8.2g protein; 7.3g fibre

Roasted vegetable and haloumi salad

1 medium kumara (400g), chopped coarsely
2 large carrots (360g), quartered lengthways
2 medium parsnips (500g), halved lengthways
2 cloves garlic, crushed
¼ cup (60ml) extra virgin olive oil
2 large red onions (600g), cut into wedges
4 baby eggplants (240g), halved lengthways
4 fresh long red chillies, halved
250g haloumi cheese, sliced
75g baby spinach leaves
lemon and basil dressing
½ cup (125ml) extra virgin olive oil
2 tablespoons lemon juice
¼ cup coarsely chopped fresh basil
1 teaspoon white sugar

1 Preheat oven to 220°C/200°C fan-forced.
2 Combine kumara, carrot, parsnip and half the combined garlic and olive oil on large shallow oven tray. Combine onion, eggplant, chilli and remaining oil mixture on separate shallow oven tray. Roast kumara mixture, uncovered, about 45 minutes and onion mixture, uncovered, about 30 minutes, or until vegetables are cooked and browned lightly.
3 Meanwhile, blend or process ingredients for lemon and basil dressing until smooth.
4 Just before serving, cook cheese on heated oiled grill plate until browned lightly on both sides.
5 Combine roasted vegetables with spinach; divide among serving plates. Top with cheese and drizzle with dressing.

preparation time 15 minutes **cooking time** 45 minutes **serves** 4
nutritional count per serving 53.6g total fat (12.8g saturated fat); 2880kJ (689 cal); 33.0g carbohydrate; 20.3g protein; 9.8g fibre

Roasted garlic celeriac

1 large celeriac (1.5kg)
2 tablespoons olive oil
1 medium bulb garlic (70g)
⅓ cup coarsely chopped fresh flat-leaf parsley
⅓ cup (95g) low-fat yogurt

1 Preheat oven to 180°C/160°C fan-forced. Line oven tray with baking paper.
2 Peel celeriac, cut into 3cm chunks; combine with oil in large bowl. Place celeriac and unpeeled garlic bulb on tray; roast, uncovered, turning occasionally, about 1 hour or until celeriac is tender and golden brown.
3 Cut garlic bulb in half horizontally, squeeze garlic pulp from each clove over celeriac; toss together with parsley. Serve topped with yogurt.

preparation time 15 minutes **cooking time** 1 hour **serves** 4
nutritional count per serving 10.1g total fat (1.4g saturated fat); 803kJ (192 cal); 11.0g carbohydrate; 7.0g protein; 15.5g fibre

Roasted tomatoes with garlic and herbs

9 large egg tomatoes (810g), halved
1 teaspoon sea salt
1 teaspoon cracked black pepper
8 sprigs fresh thyme
2 cloves garlic, sliced thinly
¼ cup (60ml) olive oil
2 teaspoons finely chopped fresh oregano
1 teaspoon finely chopped fresh thyme

1 Preheat oven to 200°C/180°C fan-forced.
2 Place tomatoes, cut-side up, in single layer, in large baking dish. Sprinkle with combined salt, pepper, thyme sprigs, garlic and 1 tablespoon of the oil; roast, uncovered, about 1 hour or until tomato softens and browns lightly.
3 Drizzle tomato with combined chopped herbs and remaining oil.

preparation time 10 minutes **cooking time** 1 hour **serves** 6
nutritional count per serving 9.3g total fat (1.3g saturated fat); 426kJ (102 cal); 2.7g carbohydrate; 1.4g protein; 1.8g fibre
tip roast the tomatoes in a baking dish with deep sides; this shields them from the heat so they won't burn.

Rosemary potatoes

3kg desiree potatoes
2 tablespoons olive oil
1 tablespoon fresh rosemary leaves

1 Preheat oven to 180°C/160°C fan-forced.
2 Make 1cm cuts in each potato, slicing about three-quarters of the way through.
3 Combine potatoes with oil in large baking dish, sprinkle with salt and freshly ground black pepper. Roast about 1 hour.
4 Increase oven temperature to 220°C/200°C fan-forced. Roast potatoes further 15 minutes or until browned and tender. Sprinkle with rosemary.

preparation time 20 minutes **cooking time** 1 hour 15 minutes
serves 10
nutritional count per serving 3.9g total fat (0.5g saturated fat); 807kJ (193 cal); 31.4g carbohydrate; 5.8g protein; 3.8g fibre

Roasted vegetables with harissa yogurt

1.2kg pumpkin
3 medium beetroot (500g), halved
2 medium parsnips (500g), peeled, halved lengthways
400g baby carrots, trimmed
2 medium red onions (320g), halved
2 tablespoons olive oil
50g butter, chopped
1 cup (280g) greek-style yogurt
1 tablespoon harissa

1 Preheat oven to 220°C/200°C fan-forced.
2 Cut pumpkin into thin wedges. Place all vegetables in two large baking dishes; drizzle with oil and dot with butter.
3 Roast vegetables, uncovered, 40 minutes, turning once. Remove vegetables as they are cooked; return trays to oven further 10 minutes or until all vegetables are browned and tender.
4 Meanwhile, combine yogurt and harissa in a small bowl.
5 Serve roasted vegetables with harissa yogurt.

preparation 15 minutes **cooking time** 50 minutes **serves** 6
nutritional count per serving 17.2g total fat (8.0g saturated fat);
1471kJ (352 cal); 35.0g carbohydrate; 10.0g protein; 8.6g fibre
tip harissa is a red chilli paste from Tunisia. Many varieties are hot, but we used quite a mild variety. It is available from gourmet food stores and delicatessens.

Mixed garlic mushrooms

500g flat mushrooms
⅓ cup (80ml) extra virgin olive oil
500g swiss brown mushrooms
500g button mushrooms
2 cloves garlic, sliced thinly
½ cup loosely packed flat-leaf parsley leaves

1 Preheat oven to 200°C/180°C fan-forced.
2 Place flat mushrooms in large baking dish, drizzle with half of the oil; roast, uncovered, 10 minutes.
3 Add remaining mushrooms, oil and garlic to dish; roast, uncovered, further 15 minutes or until mushrooms are tender and browned lightly. Stir in parsley.

preparation time 5 minutes **cooking time** 25 minutes **serves** 10
nutritional count per serving 7.8g total fat (1.0g saturated fat); 418kJ (100 cal); 0.5g carbohydrate; 5.5g protein; 4.0g fibre

Goat-cheese-stuffed roast capsicum with tapenade

4 medium red capsicums (800g)
300g firm goat cheese
200g fresh ricotta cheese
2 tablespoons sour cream
2 tablespoons extra virgin olive oil
1 tablespoon small basil leaves
tapenade
1 tablespoon drained capers
3 drained anchovy fillets
½ cup (60g) seeded black olives
1 tablespoon lemon juice
¼ cup (60ml) extra virgin olive oil

1 Preheat oven to 240°C/220°C fan-forced.
2 Place capsicums on oiled oven tray; roast, uncovered, about 15 minutes or until skin blisters and blackens. Cover capsicum with plastic or paper for 5 minutes; peel away skin. Slice off and discard top and bottom of capsicums; carefully remove and discard seeds and membrane from inside remaining capsicum pieces. Trim capsicum pieces to 8cm in depth; cut each in half to make two 4cm "rings" (you will have eight rings).
3 Blend or process cheeses and sour cream until smooth. Fit one capsicum ring inside a 5.5cm-round cutter, place on serving plate, spoon cheese mixture inside capsicum ring; carefully remove cutter. Repeat with remaining capsicum and cheese mixture.
4 Blend or process ingredients for tapenade until smooth.
5 Serve capsicum with tapenade, drizzle with oil, sprinkle with basil and freshly ground black pepper.

preparation time 30 minutes
cooking time 20 minutes (plus standing time) **serves** 8
nutritional count per serving 22.5g total fat (8.7g saturated fat); 1104kJ (264 cal); 6.1g carbohydrate; 9.5g protein; 1.1g fibre
tip the name tapenade derives from tapeno, the Provençal word for capers, a vital ingredient in this tangy condiment that perfectly complements goat cheese.

Roasted tomatoes with balsamic dressing

12 large egg tomatoes (1kg), halved lengthways
⅓ cup (80ml) olive oil
1 tablespoon white sugar
2 cloves garlic, crushed
1 teaspoon salt
1 teaspoon cracked black pepper
1 tablespoon balsamic vinegar
1 tablespoon shredded fresh basil leaves

1 Preheat oven to 180°C/160°C fan-forced.
2 Place tomato, cut-side up, on oiled wire rack in baking dish. Brush with half of the combined oil, sugar, garlic, salt and pepper. Roast, uncovered, about 1½ hours or until tomato is softened and browned lightly.
3 Drizzle combined remaining oil mixture and vinegar over tomatoes; scatter with basil.

preparation time 10 minutes **cooking time** 1 hour 30 minutes **serves** 6
nutritional count per serving 12.3g total fat (1.7g saturated fat);
523kJ (137 cal); 4.0g carbohydrate; 1.7g protein; 2.2g fibre

Baked potatoes

The perfect baked potato should be salty and crisp on the outside and snow white and fluffy on the inside. You can also use russet burbank or spunta potatoes for this recipe.

8 king edward potatoes (1.4kg), unpeeled

1 Preheat oven to 180°C/160°C fan-forced.
2 Pierce skin of each potato with fork; wrap each potato in foil, place on oven tray. Bake 1 hour or until tender. Top with one of the variations below.

preparation time 5 minutes **cooking time** 1 hour **makes** 8
nutritional count per potato 0.2g total fat (0.0g saturated fat); 493kJ (118 cal); 22.9g carbohydrate; 4.2g protein; 3.5g fibre

Toppings
cream cheese and pesto combine ⅔ cup spreadable cream cheese, ½ teaspoon cracked black pepper and ⅓ cup pesto in small bowl; refrigerate until required.
preparation time 5 minutes **makes** 8
nutritional count per potato 11.3g total fat (5.2g saturated fat); 966kJ (231 cal); 23.6g carbohydrate; 7.0g protein; 3.8g fibre

lime and chilli yogurt combine ⅔ cup yogurt, 2 tablespoons coarsely chopped fresh coriander, 2 fresh small seeded finely chopped red thai chillies and 1 teaspoon finely grated lime rind in small bowl; refrigerate until required.
preparation time 5 minutes **makes** 8
nutritional count per potato 1.0g total fat (0.5g saturated fat); 564kJ (135 cal); 24.1g carbohydrate; 5.3g protein; 3.5g fibre

mustard and walnut butter mash 60g softened butter, 1 teaspoon wholegrain mustard and 2 tablespoons finely chopped toasted walnuts in small bowl until mixture forms a paste; refrigerate until required.
preparation time 5 minutes **makes** 8
nutritional count per potato 7.9g total fat (4.1g saturated fat); 790kJ (189 cal); 23.1g carbohydrate; 4.6g protein; 3.7g fibre

Toppings left to right: cream cheese and pesto, lime and chilli yogurt, mustard and walnut butter

Mustard and honey-glazed roasted kumara

2.5kg kumara, unpeeled
⅔ cup (240g) honey
⅓ cup (95g) wholegrain mustard
2 tablespoons coarsely chopped fresh rosemary

1 Preheat oven to 220°C/200°C fan-forced.
2 Halve kumara lengthways; cut each half into 2cm wedges.
3 Combine kumara with remaining ingredients in large bowl. Divide kumara mixture between two large shallow baking dishes. Roast, uncovered, about 1 hour or until kumara is tender and slightly caramelised.

preparation time 10 minutes **cooking time** 1 hour **serves** 8
nutritional count per serving 0.6g total fat (0.0g saturated fat);
1229kJ (294 cal); 62.8g carbohydrate; 5.8g protein; 5.3g fibre

Chipped potatoes with malt vinegar

5 medium potatoes (1kg)
1 tablespoon olive oil
2 egg whites, beaten lightly
⅓ cup (80ml) brown malt vinegar

1 Preheat oven to 220°C/200°C fan-forced.
2 Slice potatoes thinly. Toss potato in combined oil and egg white. Place potato mixture, in single layer, in oiled baking dish; sprinkle with salt and freshly ground black pepper.
3 Roast potato, uncovered, about 30 minutes or until potato is golden and crisp. Serve drizzled with malt vinegar.

preparation time 15 minutes **cooking time** 30 minutes **serves** 6
nutritional count per serving 3.2g total fat (0.4g saturated fat); 497kJ (119 cal); 17.5g carbohydrate; 4.0g protein; 2.1g fibre

glossary

allspice also called pimento or jamaican pepper; so-named as it tastes like a combination of nutmeg, cumin, clove and cinnamon. Available whole or ground.

almonds

blanched brown skins removed.

meal ground almonds.

slivered small pieces cut lengthways.

artichokes

globe large flower-bud of a member of the thistle family; it has tough petal-like leaves, and is edible in part when cooked.

jerusalem neither from Jerusalem nor an artichoke, this crunchy brown-skinned tuber tastes a bit like a water chestnut and belongs to the sunflower family. Eaten raw in salads or cooked like potatoes.

bacon rashers also called bacon slices.

barley, pearl has had the husk removed then hulled and polished so that only the "pearl" of the original grain remains, much the same as white rice.

beans

black also known as turtle beans, are Cuban or Latin American rather than Chinese in origin. Jet black with a tiny white eye, black beans can be found, either packaged or loose, in most greengrocers and delicatessens.

kidney medium-sized red bean, slightly floury in texture yet sweet in flavour. Available dried or canned.

soy the most nutritious of all legumes. High in protein and low in carbohydrates, and the source of products such as tofu, soy milk, soy sauce, tamari and miso. Sometimes sold fresh as edamame; also available dried and canned.

beetroot also known as beets.

breadcrumbs

fresh bread, often white, processed into crumbs.

packaged prepared fine-textured, crunchy white breadcrumbs.

stale crumbs made by grating, blending or processing 1- or 2-day-old bread.

broccolini a cross between broccoli and chinese kale; long asparagus-like stems with a long loose floret, both completely edible. Resembles broccoli, but is milder and sweeter.

buk choy also known as bok choy, pak choi, chinese white cabbage or chinese chard; has a fresh, mild mustard taste. Use both stems and leaves. Baby buk choy, also known as pak kat farang or shanghai bok choy, is much smaller and more tender.

burghul also known as bulghur wheat; hulled

steamed wheat kernels that, once dried, are crushed into various sized grains. Used in Middle Eastern dishes such as felafel, kibbeh and tabbouleh. Burghul is not the same thing as cracked wheat, the untreated whole wheat berry broken during milling into a cereal product of varying degrees of coarseness.

butter we use salted butter unless stated otherwise.

buttermilk in spite of its name, it is actually low in fat. Originally the term given to the slightly sour liquid left after butter was churned from cream, today it is intentionally made from no-fat or low-fat milk to which specific bacterial cultures have been added during the manufacturing process. Available from the dairy department in supermarkets.

capers sold dried and salted or pickled in a vinegar brine; baby capers are also available, both in brine or dried in salt.

capsicum also known as pepper or bell pepper.

cardamom native to India and used extensively in its cuisine; available in pod, seed or ground form. Has a distinctive aromatic, sweetly rich flavour and is one of the world's most expensive spices.

cayenne pepper is a thin-fleshed, long, extremely hot, dried red chilli, usually ground.

celeriac tuberous root with knobbly brown skin, white flesh and a celery-like flavour. Keep peeled celeriac in acidulated water to stop it from discolouring before use.

char siu sauce also known as Chinese barbecue sauce; a paste-like ingredient that is dark-red-brown in colour and possesses a sharp sweet and spicy flavour. Made with fermented soybeans, honey and spices.

cheese

fetta Greek in origin; a crumbly textured goat- or sheep-milk cheese having a sharp, salty taste. Ripened and stored in salted whey.

goat made from goat milk, has an earthy, strong taste. Available in soft, crumbly and firm textures, in various shapes and sizes, and sometimes rolled in ash or herbs.

haloumi Greek in origin; a crumbly textured goat- or sheep-milk cheese having a sharp, salty taste. Ripened and stored in salted whey.

parmesan also called parmigiano, parmesan is a hard, grainy cow-milk cheese which originated in the Parma region of Italy. The curd for this cheese is salted in brine for a month before being aged for up to 2 years, preferably in humid conditions.

pizza a commercial blend of varying proportions of processed grated mozzarella, cheddar and parmesan.

ricotta a soft, sweet, moist, white cow-milk cheese with a low fat content (about 8.5%) and a slightly grainy texture.

chilli use rubber gloves when seeding and chopping fresh chillies as they can burn your skin. We use seeded chillies in our recipes as the seeds contain the heat; use fewer chillies rather than seeding the lot.

red thai also called "scuds"; tiny and very hot.

chinese cooking wine also called shao hsing or chinese rice wine; made from fermented rice, wheat, sugar and salt with a 13.5 per cent alcohol content. Inexpensive and found in Asian food shops; if you can't find it, replace with mirin or sherry.

chorizo sausage of Spanish origin, made of coarsely ground pork and highly seasoned with garlic and chilli.

choy sum also called pakaukeo or flowering cabbage, a member of the buk choy family. Has long stems, light green leaves and yellow flowers; both stems and leaves are edible.

cinnamon available as sticks (quills) and ground into powder; one of the world's most common spices, used universally as a sweet, fragrant flavouring in both sweet and savoury dishes.

cloves dried flower buds of a tropical tree; can be used whole or in ground form. They have a strong scent and taste so should be used sparingly.

coconut milk not the liquid inside the fruit (coconut water), but the diluted liquid from the second pressing of the white flesh of a mature coconut. Available in cans and cartons at most supermarkets.

coriander also known as cilantro, pak chee or chinese parsley; bright-green-leafed herb with a pungent aroma and taste. Coriander seeds are dried and sold whole or ground, and neither form tastes remotely like the fresh leaf.

cornflour also called cornstarch. Made from corn or wheat.

couscous a fine, grain-like cereal product made from semolina; from the countries of North Africa. It is rehydrated by steaming or with the addition of a warm liquid and swells to three or four times its original size.

crème fraîche a mature, naturally fermented cream (min. 35 per cent fat content) with a velvety texture and slightly tangy, nutty flavour. A French variation of sour cream, it can boil without curdling and is used in sweet and savoury dishes.

cumin also called zeera or comino and resembles caraway in size; is the dried seed of a plant related to the parsley family.

eggplant also known as aubergine.

fennel also known as finocchio or anise; a crunchy green vegetable slightly resembling celery. Also the name given to the dried seeds of the plant which have a stronger licorice flavour.

fish sauce called naam pla (Thail) or nuoc naam (Vietnamese); the two are almost identical. Made from pulverised salted fermented fish (most often anchovies); has a pungent smell and strong taste. Available in varying degrees of intensity, so use according to your taste.

five-spice powder ingredients may vary, but is most often a mixture of ground cinnamon, cloves, star anise, sichuan pepper and fennel seeds.

flour, plain also called all-purpose flour.

gai lan also known as gai larn, chinese broccoli and chinese kale; green vegetable appreciated more for its stems than its coarse leaves.

garam masala literally meaning blended spices in its northern Indian place of origin; based on varying proportions of cardamom, cinnamon, cloves, coriander, fennel and cumin, roasted and ground together.

ghee clarified butter; with milk solids removed, this fat can be heated to a high temperature without burning.

ginger

fresh also known as green or root ginger; the thick gnarled root of a tropical plant.

glacé fresh ginger root preserved in sugar syrup; crystallised ginger can be substituted if rinsed with warm water and dried before using.

hoisin sauce a thick, sweet and spicy Chinese barbecue sauce made from salted fermented soybeans, onions and garlic; used as a marinade or baste, or to accent stir-fries and barbecued or roasted foods. From Asian food shops and supermarkets.

horseradish a vegetable having edible green leaves but mainly grown for its long, pungent white root. Some Asian food shops sell it fresh, but it's more common sold in bottles at the supermarket in two forms: prepared horseradish (preserved grated horseradish) and horseradish cream (a commercial creamy paste made of grated horseradish, vinegar, oil and sugar). They cannot be substituted for each other in cooking but are both used as table condiments.

juniper berries dried berries of an evergreen tree; the main flavouring ingredient in gin.

kaffir lime leaves also called bai magrood; looks like two glossy dark green leaves joined end to end, forming a rounded hourglass shape. Used fresh or dried in many South East Asian dishes, they are used like bay leaves. Sold fresh, dried or frozen, dried leaves are less potent so double the number if using as a substitute for fresh; a strip of fresh lime peel may be substituted for each kaffir lime leaf.

kalonji seeds also known as nigella or black onion seeds. Tiny, angular seeds, black on the outside and creamy within, with a sharp nutty flavour that can be enhanced by frying briefly in a dry hot pan before use. Are available in most Asian and Middle Eastern food shops. Often called black cumin seeds.

kecap manis a dark, thick sweet soy sauce.

kumara the polynesian name of an orange-fleshed sweet potato often confused with yam.

lemon grass a tall, clumping, lemon-smelling and tasting, sharp-edged aromatic tropical grass; the white lower part of the stem is used.

lentils (red, brown, yellow) dried pulses often identified by and named after their colour. Eaten by cultures all over the world, most famously perhaps in the dhals of India, lentils have a high food value.

maple syrup distilled from the sap of maple trees found only in Canada and parts of North America. Maple-flavoured syrup or pancake syrup is not an adequate substitute for the real thing.

mushrooms

button small, cultivated white mushrooms with a mild flavour.

oyster also known as abalone; grey-white mushrooms shaped like a fan. Prized for their smooth texture and subtle, oyster-like flavour.

shiitake *fresh*, are also called Chinese black, forest or golden oak mushrooms. Although cultivated, they have the earthiness and taste of wild mushrooms. Large and meaty, they can be used as a substitute for meat in some Asian vegetarian dishes. *Dried*, are called donko or dried Chinese mushrooms; have a unique meaty flavour. Rehydrate before use.

shimeji mild-flavoured, firm-textured variety resembling small oyster mushrooms but grown in clusters on banks of cottonseed hull. Colour fades as they mature, ranging from off-white to woody brown.

swiss brown also known as roman or cremini. Light to dark brown mushrooms with full-bodied flavour; suited for use in casseroles or being stuffed and baked.

mustard

black seeds also called brown mustard seeds; they are more pungent than the white variety.

dijon also called french; is a pale brown, creamy, distinctively flavoured, fairly mild French mustard.

wholegrain also called seeded. A French-style coarse-grain mustard made from crushed mustard seeds and dijon-style french mustard.

noodles, hokkien also known as stir-fry noodles; fresh wheat noodles resembling thick, yellow-brown spaghetti needing no pre-cooking before use.

oil

cooking spray we use a cholesterol-free cooking spray made from canola oil.

olive made from ripened olives. Extra virgin and virgin are from the first and second press, respectively, and are therefore considered the best; those labelled "extra light" or "light" refer to taste not fat levels.

peanut pressed from ground peanuts; most commonly used oil in Asian cooking because of its capacity to handle high heat without burning.

sesame made from roasted, crushed, white sesame seeds; a flavouring rather than a cooking medium.

vegetable a number of oils sourced from plant rather than animal fats.

onion

green also known as scallion or (incorrectly) shallot; an immature onion picked before the bulb has formed, having a long, bright-green edible stalk.

shallots also called french shallots, golden shallots or eschalots. Small, elongated, brown-skinned member of the onion family; they grow in tight clusters similar to garlic.

spring crisp, narrow green-leafed tops and a round sweet white bulb larger than green onions.

oyster sauce Asian in origin, this thick, richly flavoured brown sauce is made from oysters and their brine, cooked with salt and soy sauce, and thickened with starches.

pancetta an Italian unsmoked bacon, pork belly cured in salt and spices then rolled into a sausage shape and dried for several weeks. Used, sliced or chopped, as an ingredient rather than eaten on its own.

paprika ground dried sweet red capsicum. Hot, smoked, sweet and mild are some of many grades and types available.

pecans native to the US and now grown locally; pecans are golden brown, buttery and rich. Good in savoury as well as sweet dishes; walnuts are a good substitute.

pepitas pale green kernels of dried pumpkin seeds; they can be bought plain or salted.

pine nuts also known as pignoli; not in fact a nut but a small, cream-coloured kernel from pine cones. They are best roasted before use to bring out the flavour.

polenta also called cornmeal; a flour-like cereal made of dried corn (maize). Also the name of the dish made from it.

potatoes

baby new also called chats; not a separate variety but an early harvest with very thin skin. Good unpeeled steamed, eaten hot or cold in salads.

desiree oval, smooth and pink-skinned, waxy yellow flesh; good in salads, boiled and roasted.

kipfler small, finger-shaped, nutty flavour; great baked and in salads.

nicola medium-sized, oval, beige skin, yellow flesh; good for mashing.

russet burbank also known as idaho; russet in colour, great baked.

sebago white skin, oval; good fried, mashed and baked.

prosciutto a kind of unsmoked Italian ham; salted, air-cured and aged, it is usually eaten uncooked.

quail small, delicate-flavoured game birds ranging in weight from 250g to 300g; also known as partridge.

rice

arborio small, round grain rice well-suited to absorb a large amount of liquid; the high level of starch makes it especially suitable for risottos, giving the dish its classic creaminess.

basmati a white, fragrant long-grained rice, the grains fluff up when cooked; wash several times before cooking.

risoni small rice-shape pasta; very similar to orzo.

rocket also known as arugula, rugula and rucola; peppery green leaf eaten raw in salads or used in cooking. Baby rocket leaves are smaller and less peppery.

saffron stigma of a member of the crocus family, available ground or in strands; imparts a yellow-orange colour to food once infused. The quality can vary greatly; the best is the most expensive spice in the world.

sambal oelek also ulek or olek; Indonesian in origin, this is a salty paste made from ground chillies and vinegar.

sesame seeds black and white are the most common of this small oval seed, however there are also red and brown varieties. A good source of calcium, the seeds are used in cuisines the world over as an ingredient and as a condiment. To toast, spread the seeds in a heavy-base frying pan; toast briefly over low heat.

sichuan peppercorns also called szechuan or Chinese pepper; a mildly hot spice. Although not related to the peppercorn family, its small, red-brown aromatic berries do look like black peppercorns and have a distinctive peppery-lemon flavour and aroma.

soy sauce also called sieu; made from fermented soybeans. Several varieties are available in supermarkets and Asian food stores; we use Japanese soy sauce unless stated otherwise.

spatchcock a small chicken (poussin), no more than 6 weeks old, weighing a maximum of 500g. Also, a cooking term to describe splitting a small chicken open, then flattening and grilling.

spinach also known as english spinach and, incorrectly, silverbeet. Baby spinach leaves are eaten raw in salads; larger leaves can be cooked until just wilted.

star anise a dried star-shaped pod; its seeds have an astringent aniseed flavour.

sugar

brown extremely soft, fine granulated sugar retaining molasses for its characteristic colour and flavour.

caster also known as superfine or finely granulated table sugar. The fine crystals dissolve easily so it is perfect for cakes, meringues and desserts.

palm also called nam tan pip, jaggery, jawa or gula melaka; made from the sap of the sugar palm tree. Light brown to black in colour and usually sold in rock-hard

cakes; use brown sugar if unavailable.

sumac a purple-red, astringent spice ground from berries growing on shrubs that flourish wild around the Mediterranean; adds a tart, lemony flavour to dips and dressings and goes well with barbecued meat. Can be found in Middle Eastern food stores.

tahini sesame seed paste available from Middle Eastern food stores; most often used in hummus and baba ghanoush.

tamarind the tamarind tree produces clusters of hairy brown pods, each of which is filled with seeds and a viscous pulp, that are dried and pressed into the blocks of tamarind found in Asian food shops. Has a sweet-sour, slightly astringent taste.

concentrate the commercial result of the distillation of tamarind juice into a condensed, compacted paste.

tat soi a variety of buk choy, developed to grow close to the ground so it is easily protected from frost.

tomatoes

cherry also known as tiny tim or tom thumb tomatoes; small and round.

egg also called plum or roma, these are smallish,

oval-shaped tomatoes much used in Italian cooking or salads.

paste triple-concentrated tomato puree used to flavour soups, stews, sauces and casseroles.

turmeric also called kamin; a rhizome related to galangal and ginger. Must be grated or pounded to release its acrid aroma and pungent flavour. Known for the golden colour it imparts, fresh turmeric can be substituted with the more common dried powder.

vinegar

balsamic originally from Modena, Italy, there are now many balsamic vinegars on the market ranging in pungency and quality depending on how, and for how long, they have been aged. Quality can be determined up to a point by price; use the most expensive sparingly.

brown malt made from fermented malt and beech shavings.

cider made from fermented apples.

raspberry made from fresh raspberries steeped in a white wine vinegar.

worcestershire sauce thin, dark-brown spicy sauce developed by the British when in India.

yogurt we use plain full-cream yogurt unless stated otherwise.

zucchini also known as courgette.

index

conversion chart

MEASURES

One Australian metric measuring cup holds approximately 250ml, one Australian metric tablespoon holds 20ml, one Australian metric teaspoon holds 5ml.

The difference between one country's measuring cups and another's is within a two- or three-teaspoon variance, and will not affect your cooking results.North America, New Zealand and the United Kingdom use a 15ml tablespoon.

All cup and spoon measurements are level. The most accurate way of measuring dry ingredients is to weigh them. When measuring liquids, use a clear glass or plastic jug with the metric markings.

We use large eggs with an average weight of 60g.

LIQUID MEASURES

METRIC	IMPERIAL
30ml	1 fluid oz
60ml	2 fluid oz
100ml	3 fluid oz
125ml	4 fluid oz
150ml	5 fluid oz (¼ pint/1 gill)
190ml	6 fluid oz
250ml	8 fluid oz
300ml	10 fluid oz (½ pint)
500ml	16 fluid oz
600ml	20 fluid oz (1 pint)
1000ml (1 litre)	1¾ pints

LENGTH MEASURES

METRIC	IMPERIAL
3mm	⅛in
6mm	¼in
1cm	½in
2cm	¾in
2.5cm	1in
5cm	2in
6cm	2½in
8cm	3in
10cm	4in
13cm	5in
15cm	6in
18cm	7in
20cm	8in
23cm	9in
25cm	10in
28cm	11in
30cm	12in (1ft)

DRY MEASURES

METRIC	IMPERIAL
15g	½oz
30g	1oz
60g	2oz
90g	3oz
125g	4oz (¼lb)
155g	5oz
185g	6oz
220g	7oz
250g	8oz (½lb)
280g	9oz
315g	10oz
345g	11oz
375g	12oz (¾lb)
410g	13oz
440g	14oz
470g	15oz
500g	16oz (1lb)
750g	24oz (1½lb)
1kg	32oz (2lb)

OVEN TEMPERATURES

These oven temperatures are only a guide for conventional ovens.
For fan-forced ovens, check the manufacturer's manual.

	°C (CELSIUS)	°F (FAHRENHEIT)	GAS MARK
Very slow	120	250	½
Slow	150	275 – 300	1 – 2
Moderately slow	160	325	3
Moderate	180	350 – 375	4 – 5
Moderately hot	200	400	6
Hot	220	425 – 450	7 – 8
Very hot	240	475	9

General manager Christine Whiston
Editorial director Susan Tomnay
Creative director Hieu Chi Nguyen
Editor Stephanie Kistner
Designer Caryl Wiggins
Food director Pamela Clark
Recipe consultant Louise Patniotis
Associate food editor Alex Somerville
Nutritional information Rebecca Squadrito
Director of sales Brian Cearnes
Marketing manager Bridget Cody
Business analyst Ashley Davies
Operations manager David Scotto
International rights enquires Laura Bamford
lbamford@acpuk.com

ACP Books are published by ACP Magazines
a division of PBL Media Pty Limited
Group publisher, Women's lifestyle Pat Ingram
Director of sales, Women's lifestyle Lynette Phillips
Commercial manager, Women's lifestyle Seymour Cohen
Marketing director, Women's lifestyle Matthew Dominello
Public relations manager, Women's lifestyle Hannah Deveraux
Creative director, Events, Women's lifestyle Luke Bonnano
Research Director, Women's lifestyle Justin Stone
ACP Magazines, Chief Executive officer Scott Lorson
PBL Media, Chief Executive officer Ian Law

Produced by ACP Books, Sydney.
Published by ACP Books, a division of ACP Magazines Ltd.
54 Park St, Sydney NSW Australia 2000. GPO Box 4088, Sydney, NSW 2001.
Phone +61 2 9282 8618 Fax +61 2 9267 9438
acpbooks@acpmagazines.com.au www.acpbooks.com.au
Printed by Toppan Printing Co, China.

Australia Distributed by Network Services, GPO Box 4088, Sydney, NSW 2001.
Phone +61 2 9282 8777 Fax +61 2 9264 3278 networkweb@networkservicescompany.com.au
United Kingdom Distributed by Australian Consolidated Press (UK),
10 Scirocco Close, Moulton Park Office Village, Northampton, NN3 6AP.
Phone +44 1604 642 200 Fax +44 1604 642 300
books@acpuk.com www.acpuk.com
New Zealand Distributed by Netlink Distribution Company, ACP Media Centre, Cnr Fanshawe
and Beaumont Streets, Westhaven, Auckland. PO Box 47906, Ponsonby, Auckland, NZ.
Phone +64 9 366 9966 Fax 0800 277 412 ask@ndc.co.nz
South Africa Distributed by PSD Promotions, 30 Diesel Road Isando, Gauteng Johannesburg.
PO Box 1175, Isando 1600, Gauteng Johannesburg.
Phone +27 11 392 6065/6/7 Fax +27 11 392 6079/80 orders@psdprom.co.za

Clark, Pamela.
The Australian women's weekly roast
Includes index.
ISBN 978-1-86396-753-2 (pbk)
1. Roasting (Cookery).
I. Clark, Pamela.
641.71
© ACP Magazines Ltd 2008
ABN 18 053 273 546
This publication is copyright. No part of it may be reproduced or
transmitted in any form without the written permission of the publishers.

To order books, phone 136 116 (within Australia).
Send recipe enquiries to: recipeenquiries@acpmagazines.com.au

Cover Spring roast lamb with mint sauce, p152
Photographer Tanya Zouev
Stylist Jane Hann
Food preparation Arianne Bradshaw
Illustrations Hannah Blackmore
Acknowledgments Prop Stop